From Polders
to Postmodernism

From Polders to Postmodernism

A Concise History of Archival Theory

By John Ridener

Litwin Books, LLC
Duluth, Minnesota

Copyright 2008 John Ridener

Published in 2009

Litwin Books, LLC
PO Box 3320
Duluth MN 55803

http://litwinbooks.com/

ISBN 978-0-9802004-5-4

Printed on acid-free paper that meets current ANSI standards for archival preservation.

Library of Congress Cataloging-in-Publication Data

Ridener, John.
 From Polders to postmodernism : a concise history of archival theory / by John Ridener.
    p. cm.
 Includes bibliographical references and index.
 Summary: "A history of the conception and development of the theories that have guided archivists in their work from the late 19th through the early 21st centuries"--Provided by publisher.
 ISBN 978-0-9802004-5-4 (alk. paper)
 1. Archives--Administration--History. 2. Archives--Administration. I. Title.
 CD947.R54 2009
 027.001--dc22
                                    2008042286

For JBP

&

(CPR)

Contents

	Acknowledgments	ix
	Foreword by Terry Cook	xi
1.	Why Study Archival Theory?	1
2.	Contexts	7
3.	Consolidation: The Dutch Manual	21
4.	Confirmation and Reinforcement: Sir Hilary Jenkinson's *A Manual of Archive Administration*	41
5.	Modern Records: T. R. Schellenberg and *Modern Archives*	69
6.	Questioning Archives: Contemporary Records, Contemporary Discourses	101
7.	From Polders to Postmodernism	143
	References	163
	Index	175
	About the Author	185

Acknowledgments

No written work is the product of only the author's efforts. This book is no exception. Of course, all errors and omissions in the text are my own.

The following individuals deserve much more than the thanks given here:

Rory Litwin, of Litwin Books, who asked if I would be interested in revising my thesis for publication and who has been a steady guide through that process even when I sought to push the boundaries of his effort.

Professors Debbie Hansen, Lori Lindberg, and Judy Weedman all of the San Jose State School of Library and Information Science, who agreed, possibly against their better judgment, to be my thesis committee for a year and a half when "no one" writes a thesis in library school. Your patience, eagerness to teach, and willingness to explore new ideas has been instrumental in the development of this book.

Those who commented on the manuscript: Todd Neece, whose constant intellectual curiosity and erudition serve as an inspiration for us all; Cody Hennesy, whose comments on both the manuscript and librarianship are always insightful, intriguing, and correct; and Nicole Hunter, who not only gave insightful commentary on this manuscript, but also whose perspective helped transform some of the darkest days of library school, "checking APA," and getting to and from San Jose into a great friendship.

Bo Elder, who worked tirelessly and selflessly to edit and comment on the manuscript. Who also was eager and willing to engage with the material beyond the concepts in the book and who insightfully questioned my notions of critical theory with unparalleled deft.

My parents, Beth and Gene Ridener, who have continued to unfailingly support my oftentimes-questionable schemes regardless of how far fetched they may seem.

My wife, Jenica Babbitt-Pearce, who continues to be more amazing each day we know one another; a loving companion; when needed, a strong and thoughtful critic. And who may also not hear, "I have to work on my book" for at least a short while.

Foreword

By Terry Cook
Archival Studies Program
University of Manitoba

Writing even a short foreword for a book in which my own ideas figure significantly is no easy task. Praise the book unduly and I may appear to be rewarding the author for the positive attention paid to my work. Criticize the book too pointedly and I may seem unappreciative of that same attention, prickly over interpretations not coinciding with my own.

While it is possible both to praise and criticize John Ridener's *From Polders to Postmodernism: A Concise History of Archival Theory*, a more germane stance is simply to recommend that readers spend time with it and decide for themselves. I urge them to do so, for they will not be disappointed. This short, concise, and thoughtful volume will make them think about archives, the archive, archiving, whether as readers they be archivists or other record professionals on the inside of the profession, or scholars or researchers in other disciplines looking in from the outside. Such thinking may well open for archivists new vistas for re-imagining their profession and their work, for understanding better their own specialized kind of archival institution or recording medium or archival function set against the broader historical landscape that Ridener paints. More profoundly, by seeing the changes Ridener sets forth in his history of the core ideas that have animated archivists in their activities over the past century, archivists should appreciate better the social, cultural, technological, and paradigmatic contingencies of their own work. They will accordingly reject, if they read Ridener well, any lingering notions of universal laws and positivist theories being appropriate for today's archives and the complex and pluralistic societies they serve (and should reflect). For those in other disciplines engaged in exploring the "archive" (singular), seeing the evolution of the ideas over time and across space articulated by real live archivists inside real operational "archives" (plural) will be enlightening; it is those archivists, after all is said and done, who actually create the archive that remains for those scholars to consider.

Of course, it is easy to criticize any work self-described in its title as "concise." Some archivists will disagree with the choices the author has made of what and who to analyze, and through which secondary writers those perceptions are gained. The field of archival theory – as ideas and concepts, existing in themselves and evolving over time – is vast, complex, and problematic. Ridener is evidently not able to include all possible thinkers or ideas relevant to his large theme in a short book. Where are Richard Cox or Barbara Craig on appraisal theory; or Tom Nesmith or (save for one of many prolific works) Verne Harris on the postmodern archive; or Sue McKemmish or Catherine Hobbs on personal/private archives; or such major figures as Hugh Taylor or David Bearman on many themes? Ridener's approach, then, embraces the very subjectivity of history, as he locates some representative thinkers to illuminate the changing paradigms he is analyzing, rather than tries to summarize all contemporary archival theoreticians. The approach focuses on the paradigms, with no pretense at being a comprehensive history of archival theory. The book is all the stronger for its lean focus, even if one may object to some inclusions and other omissions.

In this, Ridener has had to make some hard choices, exercise judgement, make selections, focus on some ideas and thinkers and ignore others, in order to push his narrative along. He has had, in short, to make appraisal decisions about what is important and what is not, about what is most representative of his themes and what is not. The result is a very approachable entrée to the various theories, concepts, ideas, and assumptions that have animated archivists collectively over the past century in the English-speaking world, but one that will certainly generate some "why didn't he include this" as well as vigorous nods of agreement along the lines of "now that's something I hadn't thought of before."

The archival function of appraisal is in fact central to Ridener's analysis as much as to his method. One might suggest that the book, despite its title, is less about "archival theory" than about "appraisal theory." While Ridener is certainly sensitive to the reality that the first codifications of archival theory by Dutch and English archivists before 1930 focussed on ideas about the arrangement and description of records, and ignored appraisal as we understand that function today, he still sees these early writers' ideas through the prism of appraisal. And his analysis of the core ideas after 1930 is almost exclusively focused on appraisal. Yet "archival theory" encompasses much more than appraisal. There is voluminous literature on the ideas, concepts, and high-level strategies (all of which I would term "theory," as contrasted to practice and methodology) that address the evidential characteristics of records, arrangement and description, public programming, preservation, each archival recording medium from maps to photography to film, and of course computer-generated records and the digital evolution, to say nothing of the personal archive and personal record creators virtually ignored here.

Yet there is a logic to Ridener's choice. Appraisal is *the* critical archival act by archivists. Helen Samuels and Richard Cox called it the archivist's "first responsibility," upon which everything else depends. As archivists appraise records, they are determining what the future will know about its past: who will have a continuing voice and who will be silenced. Archivists thereby co-create the archive. Archival appraisal decides which creators, functions, and activities generating records in society will be represented in archives, by defining, identifying, then selecting which documents and which media become archives in the first place. Appraisal is also the gateway function to all subsequent archival activity. Once records are appraised as having archival value and are acquired or protected by the archival institution, even being in that privileged state does not ensure equal treatment thereafter. They are continually appraised and reappraised for their "value" when the archivist decides, against the realities of huge backlogs, limited resources, and pressing user, external, and professional demands, which records are to enjoy all, many, or only some limited dimensions of numerous subsequent archival processes, more or less in the following sequential order: re-ordering into more "logical" arrangements and groupings the records that have been appraised and acquired as archival; providing varying levels of technical processing for machine-dependent audio-visual film and sound archives and for computer-generated digital records; analyzing series or groupings of records to highlight the salient people, places, ideas, and events, in the mere paragraph or two of a typical archival description for a series of records that may contain a million pages or thousands of images; creating for some records more detailed catalogues, listings, or finding aids or specialized or thematic guides; furnishing conservation services and stabilization of the physical recording media; implementing migration programs (especially for audio-visual and digital records) to new storage media and new reading/software platforms as old environments deteriorate or become obsolete; copying for preservation by microfilming or digital scanning; and finally – and the function most directly visible to researchers – deciding (through many complex processes, including the archivist's own education and experience) which of all these already heavily filtered records (by these previous interventions, or lack thereof) should now be featured in exhibitions, publications, educational outreach programs, and specialized reference services, or selected to be included in on-line finding aids, as digitized images of documents, and for virtual exhibitions, to be accessible to everyone everywhere. In a way then, since every archival function requires the archivist to appraise the value, worth, significance, and impact of the proposed action (or inaction) that the archives may take, in a very real way appraisal is the *only* archival function, never ending, always opening to new possibilities. In that sense, Ridener's insight equating archival and appraisal theory has considerable merit, for the archivist is continually assigning and re-assigning value.

But appraisal more narrowly defined, as the keep-or-destroy decision of what records the archives actually acquires, what becomes/defines the archive, not only places some records, and their creators (and the functions and activities in which they were engaged), on the memory pedestal, but also, starkly and with finality, decides which records are to be destroyed, excluded from archives and from all these subsequent archival functions, processes, and enhancements, thus effectually removed from societal memory. By the appraisal process, to come to the harsh reality, about 1 to 5 percent of the total available documentation of major institutions and governments is preserved as archives, and an even smaller percentage from the totality of records of all possible private citizens, groups, and organizations.

Appraisal as a function thus challenges most fundamentally both historians' stereotypes and archivists' mythologies about the archivist's role in society. If archivists are now rarely depicted as aged and bearded antiquarians stooped over dusty ledgers, they are certainly not generally acknowledged as people constructing social memory to meet/reflect contemporary needs, values, and assumptions; that is the role of historians and other users of the archive. Rather, the archivist is still widely perceived as a kind of honest broker between the creators of records and the records' later use by researchers, including historians. This view is not surprising, since early archival theorists depicted themselves, as Ridener well illustrates, as just such guardians and passive curators of the documentary past, not as its on-going interpreters or mediators. Indeed, archivists in Britain until very recently were called "keepers" to reflect this very mindset; in Canada, archivists until the 1980s were seen as "handmaidens of historians." Canada's first Dominion Archivist opined that the work he did in arranging archival records was "purely mechanical," requiring "no special qualifications." Underlying these stereotypes and mythologies was an earnest quest, by archivists and historians alike, for objectivity, for impartiality, for Truth, all extolled as self-defining professional virtues, but, alas, in reality, all an impossible dream in light of the inescapable subjectivity that any value-creating and value-enforcing activity such as archival appraisal must always entail.

This traditional curatorial and neutered mindset of the impartial archivist is fundamentally and convincingly challenged by John Ridener as he exposes the on-going tension historically between objectivity and subjectivity. He sets his analysis of archival theory in three broad periods: one of consolidation and reinforcement by 1930 of traditional archival concepts as these had evolved over the nineteenth century; the modernization of archives in the middle years of the twentieth century from 1930 to 1980 around a consensus of efficient management of cultural resources; and the collapse of that consensus by a new questioning from 1980 onwards in light of critical theory, new digital media, and awakened respect for the pluralism and many diversities in society. For each of these three periods, Ridener looks in detail at the context from which the archival ideas rose and flourished, especially changing technologies for recording information, changing contexts of work in modern government offices, changing trends in historiography to which, until very recently, archivists were closely tied, and, not least, the ever-changing personalities, backgrounds, and experiences of the archival theorists themselves. What emerges is a series of paradigmatic shifts of emphasis demonstrating convincingly that the archivist is an active agent shaping the archive, a mediator and interpreter of meaning. As I once wrote elsewhere, and Ridener demonstrates with many telling examples, "archival thinking over the century should be viewed as constantly evolving, ever mutating as it adapts to radical changes in the nature of records, record-creating organizations, record-keeping systems, record uses, and the wider cultural, legal, technological, social, and philosophical trends in society. Archival ideas formed in one time and place reflect many of these external factors, which ideas are often reconstructed, even rediscovered in another time and place, or reshaped across generations in the same place. The best archival theorists are those who have been able to recognize and articulate these radical changes in society and then deal conceptually with their impact on archival theory and practice. That articulation forms our collective discourse, the metatext or narrative animating our professional practice, and thus properly is the focus of an intellectual history of archives." John Ridener has given us a concise entry point to that complicated discourse and many stimulating insights to the intellectual history of archiving as a societal function.

Why should anyone care? What value does theory have in a profession that is very practical and methodological, focussing in its daily work on standards and consistency, on process and products. Sadly, theory and practice are too often viewed as archival polarities, rather than being complementary. I once suggested that thinking about theory and practice benefits from new concepts of performativity. Without a script, there can be no play. Without the performance of the play, the script never comes to life. Theory and practice thus cross-fertilize each other in the theatre of archives, rather than one being derivative of, or dependent on, the other, one seen as the daily reality of work, the other a professional frill or sidelight.

There is an understandable scepticism in the archival profession about theory, especially when theory can sometimes take the guise of a formulaic imposition of arcane concepts betraying little cognizance of workplace realities, or worse deteriorate into a self-indulgent quagmire of jargon-laden obfuscation. When the actors are performing in real time, under hot lights, on a very public stage, accountable to directors and sponsors, then impressing their many audiences with concrete results is what counts, not speculation of why they are doing the work.

But if *only* proceeding pragmatically – to satisfy today's users or sponsors, but without a defensible core of theoretical consistency – then the archivists/actors (and their employing institutions) are left exposed, in this era of "culture wars," to severe criticism, even ridicule, and are prone to appraising, acquiring, and preserving for posterity a poorer and less reliable record, less reflective of our contemporary society, a record equally that posterity will understand less well and use less imaginatively. When the practical work needs to be re-conceptualized, as inevitably happens when (as Ridener shows so well) new factors arise that cause accepted strategies and methodologies to break down, then theory can provide the basic principles for restructuring or re-engineering archival practice with a new and more relevant script; it can focus the justifications necessary to explain why we do what we do to our various audiences and sponsors when our results are questioned or controversial; it can enliven the vision and stimulate the professional morale necessary to unite the players/archivists around that new script and to accept the requirement for a new performance; and it can offer a self-consciousness to our performance that, as with interacting with any good theatre critic, ultimately make for better acting and better actors.

Theory thus matters. Theory defines us. Theory motivates us. Theory explains us. Theory makes for better archives and archivists. But theory is not a monolithic series of "scientific" laws objectively true in all times and places, but rather an on-going, open-ended quest for meaning about our documentary heritage that itself is ever evolving. John Ridener's *From Polders to Postmodernism: A Concise History of Archival Theory* shows this process operating in our professional past. It also suggests the prologue for our profession's future.

>Ottawa and Winnipeg
>January 2009

1. Why Study Archival Theory?

"Who controls the past controls the future: who controls the present controls the past."
—George Orwell, *Nineteen Eighty-Four*

The study of archives is the study of an applied profession. The focus of archival administration is the preservation and care of unique records of action taken by a group, government agency, organization, or company. The archive has deemed groups of records important enough to preserve in order to keep and organize the action taken by the organization. Learning to become an archivist is traditionally the study of how to perform the tasks that will make records available to future interested researchers. Therefore, much of the writing done about the profession of archives is in the form of practical application, how-to manuals and handbooks.

If being an archivist is a practical endeavor, why study archival theory? How does understanding why archives are created help an administrator who may be more concerned about budgets than with theoretical discourse? The most significant motivation to study archival theory and its development is the fact that non-archivists have challenged the definitions and meanings the archive itself. The most recent challenges come from many places including: artists and art galleries (Hunter, 2007), critical theorists (Derrida, 1995), and computer science and the Internet (Internet Archive, 2008). The new definitions of the archive include a broad and expanded sense of what it could contain and what forms it can take. Technological innovation, especially widespread use of computers, has created an expectation of democratic recordkeeping and expanded horizons for cultural memory.

If archivists are interested in participating in the interdisciplinary discourses of archival definition, knowledge of past archival theory and its transformation into contemporary theories is useful. While the meaning of the term "archive" has allowed for a range of participation in the term's definition, archivists have a vested interest in participating in defining their own profession and its location. Many concepts in archival theory, an example being *respect des fonds*, are foreign to non-professionals but may be useful and enlightening when explained in contexts more familiar to those who have engaged in defining and redefining their own meaning of the word and the institution called the "archive."

For much of their professional history, archivists have been linked with historians. As other cultural creators and critics begin to engage archivists in terms of their own profession, archivists would do well to prepare themselves to fully engage in a broad cultural discourse. To ignore the relatively new interest in the notions and definitions of the archive in favor of exclusive professional practical application is to keep one's head in the sand in hopes that archives will continue to remain vital and relatively unchanged regardless of the vagaries of engagement, cultural or otherwise. Archivists can draw on a rich and complex tradition of theory to define and redefine the archive. With a deep and critical knowledge of archival theory, archivists can be assured that their professional participation in the discourse on the meaning of the archive is communicated now and in the future.

An approach to archival theory

Archival theory has been developed with varying levels of intentionality over the past 120 years. A broad range of archives and archival situations have given rise to many theoretical approaches to keeping archives. One common thread that binds these theories together is the discourse that surrounds archival appraisal. The often-contentious disagreement regarding if and how archivists should select material to become part of archives is the key to understanding the many discourses of archival theory.

Appraisal has become so representative of archival theory that it may be difficult to conceive of a time when archivists argued over its merits. At the end of the 19th century, leading archival theorists were loath to give appraisal much influence in discussion of their theories. Eventually, this disdain for appraisal would lessen, and appraisal would become representative of the theoretical discourses within the archival profession. Especially since the 1980s, archival appraisal theory has become the focus of much professional and public discourse regarding archives. In fact, some archivists have noted that many of the articles published in the professional archival field focus on appraisal activities as the core of the archival process (Duranti, 1994). Appraisal is the initial interface between archivist and a collection: if records are appraised as less valuable than others, they may never be archived and effectively forgotten, even erased, from institutional or public memory. Luciana Duranti (1994) defines appraisal as a three-phase process "of establishing the value of documents made or received in the course of the conduct of affairs, qualifying that value, and determining its duration" (p. 329). It is easy to see why appraisal is understood to be very important to archival work, since the assignation of value, including evidentiary, juridical, and cultural, is conferred upon records during the process of appraisal. If one is able to delve deep into the controversy that surrounds the history of archival appraisal, one can understand the heart of archival theory.

But how does archival theory, as embodied by appraisal theory, operate? Is it a series of volleys between opposing schools of thought? A seesaw, back-and-forth changing-of-the-guard between those who approve of appraisal and those who deny its usefulness? Or perhaps a spectrum with individual archivists and archives at various points between completely appraised archives and archives in which nothing has been evaluated? The answer is that all of these situations are represented depending on the factors of geography, technology, and historiography. Archives hold singular information not duplicated elsewhere. It is logical that individual archives would each create their own specific approach to keeping their unique collections. How then, is one able to approach archival theory without having to map a specific, practical instance in order to understand the theoretical situation in a given archive?

This book seeks to answer that question through a close examination of the tension between subjectivity and objectivity in archival theory. That is, an understanding of how much decision-making power an individual archivist has in determining the contents of an archive. Whether one examines the theory of British archives after World War I or the contemporary electronic records held in the government archives of Canada, the one constant presence is the dialectic between an objective and a subjective approach to archives. While historians and archivists of the late nineteenth and early twentieth centuries were focused on writing history "as it happened," and keeping records that supported that specific approach to writing history, the need for archivists to have specific control over the contents of the archive has been persistent. Simultaneously, the number and types of records archivists have been charged with have increased in ever-shorter amounts of time. The history of how archivists have sought to balance material and theoretical needs while maintaining accurate evidence of action is the history of archival theory.

With an in-depth understanding of the discourse between objectivity and subjectivity in archival theory, contemporary archivists can engage with innovators, critics, and other professionals to create a broad and vital archival theory that will become and remain part of a broad cultural discourse. As technology changes rapidly, individual archivists who are aware of the discourses in archival theory will be able to draw from this knowledge and have a lasting and important impact on the shape of future archives. Understanding archival theory is crucial for archivists and archives alike.

2. Contexts

Like the writing of history, archival work is heavily influenced by the context in which that work is completed. The archive has been conceived as the repository for institutional knowledge between its usefulness as active records and its source of information for historians and researchers. Since archivists work with the products of others' work and maintain repositories for others to work from, the middle position the profession occupies creates a situation in which theories and applications from both sides deeply influence archivists and archives. In fact, one of the major concepts in archival theory, *respect des fonds*, "The principle of arrangement of archival material that records of different provenance not be intermingled" (U of T Archives & Records Management Services related information glossary, 2004), was conceived of in order to preserve the context of an organization's records as they were used when they were created.

In order to fully understand how archival theory has developed over time, it is necessary to examine the specific contexts in which each theory was created. The influences of paradigm shifts, technological changes, and shifts in historiography are all immense in the development of archival theory. Familiarity with why archivists would welcome or resist change in response to specific contextual pressures will lead to a greater understanding of how archival theory was required to change to align with each set of contemporary values and beliefs. This understanding will also illuminate not only how archivists have viewed and understood theory as part of their profession over time, but it will also show how archival theory developed from the most practical of manuals to the most theoretical statements.

Three contexts shape the creation of archival theory in general to specific ways. The first is the notion of paradigms: what they are and how and why they shift and change. The second contextual element is technological change. Records created in different media require various methods of appraisal, conservation, and storage. The nature of a record's media dictates the shape and character of the archive. The third and most influential context in which archival theory, and specifically appraisal theory, is created is that of the writing of history and historiography, the study of the writing of history. Archivists and historians have worked closely together and the work of each group continues to inform the other. Historians rely on archival material to complete their work as well as to maintain the integrity of archival records. Archivists rely on historians to use archival materials and validate the truthfulness of records in the archive. An understanding of these three contexts in which archival theory is created will illuminate many of the theoretical issues archivists have faced over time in the development of archival theories.

Paradigms

The concept of paradigm changes is very important in terms of understanding the intellectual history of archival theory. The context of paradigms and how they change is intellectual in nature rather than a social or cultural one. This book assumes the validity of paradigm changes to explain shifts and changes in archivists' approach to their work. The notions of paradigms and paradigm shifts are based on the concept of socially created knowledge, the idea that a group of individuals can agree upon shared beliefs that can be relied upon to create broadly held theories. The concept of paradigms as applied to archival theory describes, in part, how the work of a small group of people can benefit a larger, geographically dispersed group of fellow professionals. The large group benefits from and generally approves of the work of the small group of leaders whose work leads to a paradigm change.

The most well known theorist of paradigm changes is Thomas Kuhn, who established the concept of paradigms as applied to scientists in *The Structure of Scientific Revolutions* (1996/1962). In his approach to understanding the shifts in power between scientific theories, Kuhn posits that the sum of scientific knowledge is socially defined. While there are specific processes through which scientific knowledge are vetted, the result is a socially constructed agreement, a paradigm. Kuhn's approach to the changing understanding of science grants a new vocabulary with which one can begin to further an understanding of how power shifts in scientific thought.

What causes paradigms to change? In terms of archives, one reason is a crisis in the profession. This crisis requires attempts, on the part of practicing professionals, to change the dominant paradigm to answer the questions conceived during the crisis. The inability to work with new situations using old theories promotes different conceptions of both the problem and possible solutions. This is followed by a fracturing of multiple theories which all vie for acceptance. These theories are generally various in quality and plausibility, but are required to be posited in order to better represent the possibilities of new theoretical exploration. Eventually, theories are pared down as they undergo professional assessment. The surviving theories become hypotheses that allow scientists to choose between a few different approaches. Eventually, a hypothesis is proven correct and adopted by a majority of professionals. This broad adoption becomes the new paradigm.

There are notable detractors to the notion of paradigm changes and the social creation of professional standards.

The most famous anti-Kuhnian is Karl Popper (2002/1963) who argues that professional trends are the product of empirical experimentation, not mere agreement among professionals on definitions. Kuhn himself warned against the over-application of his philosophy of science. In the current context, however, the notion of the paradigm change is an apt and useful comparison in the case of the development of archival theory since not only is archival theory socially constructed knowledge, but the material archivists work with is itself socially constructed.

Technology

Another context that heavily influences the changes in archival theory is technological change. The means by which records are produced highly influences the work archivists are required to perform in order to appraise, preserve, and make those records available for use. Technological change can either significantly decrease or increase the number of records presented to the archive. For each archival paradigm, there are specific technological changes that lead, in part, to changes in archival theory.

In the Netherlands, industrialization and mechanization created a new sense of urgency in terms of efficiency and technological advance. The country was slow to industrialize before the late 19th century. Its system of waterways and reliance on wind power combined with its historical economic position as an economy based upon trade lessened the importance of industrial development in the country in favor of trade and exploration that resulted in colonization of many areas on other continents. With its historical reputation as a liberal center of trade and dependence on economies beyond its borders, the Netherlands constructed, beginning in Medieval times, a complex political structure that strove to create consensus in political decisions despite a plethora of competing opinions and interests. This inclusive approach created specialized records and evidence for archivists to preserve and make accessible.

Advances in communications technology during the last decade of the 19th century were dependent upon empirical science which influenced professional developments of all kinds (Fredericksson 2003). In terms of communications, trans-Atlantic telegraph lines lessened the importance of distance in communication and increased the speed with which individuals could communicate over long distances. Wireless radio communications were increasingly available and becoming more widely utilized to disseminate information untethered by intermediary equipment besides the radio units themselves.

During this period, as would increasingly become the case elsewhere, technological changes occurred quickly. Many of the records Dutch archivists had worked with in the past and based their theories on were Medieval, products of the country's political structure. While the professional focus for these records was on organization and preservation, the cultural zeitgeist encouraged consolidation and standardization in wake of technological changes that required specific protocols and rules such as international communication. Dutch archivists responded to this technological change with a singular and coherent archival theory. The implementation of this theory on a national level was an attempt by the authors to consolidate local practices into a contemporary archival paradigm.

Technological change continued to play a role in the establishment of archival paradigms into the early 20th century, albeit in an oppositional manner. After World War I, which illustrated the high levels of destruction made possible through the mechanization of battle, including the first use of the tank, communication technology changed quickly. The widespread use of the telephone and the standardization of the typewriter during the 1920s impacted archives by simultaneously decreasing and increasing the number and types of records presented to the archive, respectively.

The telephone created a method of communication that did not necessarily produce a written byproduct. Unless an individual took notes during a telephone conversation or used rudimentary recording devices, little or no records of a conversation or transaction existed. This created a challenge for archivists who sought to capture various details of their organization's operations.

While the telephone may have reduced the number of shorter notes and memoranda produced during the course of business, the typewriter only served to increase the number of written records for possible inclusion in the archive. With the ability to create multiple copies of documents quickly, the technological innovations wrought through the typewriter multiplied issues of duplication and authenticity for archivists who sought to preserve the most authentic documentation of an organization's actions. With the proper training and familiarity, handwritten letters and documents, especially older historical documents, could be tied to individual authors. Typewritten documents could not be identified in this manner and were, in fact, usually not committed to paper by their authors (Morton, 2000). Between the 1920s and 1950s, technological innovation would simultaneously continue to make communication easier while it made recording and saving the increasing amount of communication more difficult for archivists working in the established archival paradigm.

The post-World War II era through the 1980s was a time of unprecedented technological change. During this time, not only did technology radically change, from the use of the typewriter to organizational uses of the computer, for example, but the rate at which technology changed increased exponentially (Moore, 1965). The rapid rate of technological innovation allowed for increased organizational reliance on technological solutions to complex problems like intercontinental communication and the development of multinational corporations. The federally sponsored space exploration program also promoted technological innovation and science education in schools.

Copy machines, ubiquitous use of the typewriter, and the introduction of computer technology increased the number of records presented to the archive for preservation in ways that no archivist had foreseen. Not only did the number of records increase, but the concept of the record changed for both record creators and archivists. The ability to create records with relative ease meant more records of relatively decreasing value when compared with the records of just a few years prior. With finite resources, archivists were forced to find a way to work with unprecedented amounts of records with varied levels of meaning within them.

The meaning of the concept of the archival record itself would change with technological advances in computing from the 1980s, which continue today. As computing power and ubiquity increased, records creators and archivists alike began to rely upon them for an increasing number of tasks. Statistical analysis of organizations' actions became easier and more commonplace, creating an ever increasingly high number records and metarecords for the archive.

The acceleration of computing speed eventually would allow records to be created and used exclusively digitally. Much like the widespread use of the typewriter beginning in the 1920s, digital and electronic records created questions in regard to authenticity and duplication. Records could be created and modified by groups of people with the differentiation between original, duplicate, and version difficult if not impossible to discern. The innovation of computer technology created the need for archivists to re-conceive their theoretical assumptions concerning authorship, authenticity, and ownership of records.

Historiography

Historiography, the study of the writing of history, is the most important context in which archival theory has developed. Understanding the impact of the writing of history and the ways in which paradigms within the historical profession have shifted over time will illuminate the context of changes in archival appraisal theory. The intellectual history of archival theory is also the intellectual history of historians and historiography. As historians are required to work within the contexts of their own time as they work to understand and illuminate events of the past, archivists must work with collections that have undergone changes implemented by previous archivists working within other paradigms. For most of the relatively short history of the archival profession, archivists have themselves *been* professional historians, relied upon for their expertise in their particular specialized field of history to select records of enduring value. These archivists were trained, through their work in the historical field, to appraise records based upon their content and context. Only within the past 40 years, as archivists have begun to create their own, independent professional theories and practice, has archival theory and appraisal been separated from traditional historical practices and become a discipline unto itself.

Previous to the development of a distinct archival profession, theoretical approaches to history guided archivists' work. During the late 19th century, historians were consolidating much of their efforts into creating scientific history concerned with writing history "as it happened." This phrase was coined by a highly influential German historian,

Leopold von Ranke, who was well versed in the history of the consolidation of the Prussian empire in the 19th century. Scientific history was based on the use of primary sources, as opposed to the writings of other historians, from which historians made observations much like a scientist would make observations from empirical experiments. Ranke's historical writing, such as *Geschichte der Romanischen und Germanischen Völker von 1494 bis 1514 (History of the Latin and Teutonic Nations from 1494 to 1514)* from 1824, was guided by this theory and heralded as highly successful. Another example of this type of scientific history is *Weltbürgertum und Nationalstaat (Cosmopolitanism and the National State)* by Friedrich Meinecke. This work traced the development of nationalism in Germany during the 19th century through the archival records of the national government and used an empirical methodology to construct Germany's history during this period "as it happened." Meinecke himself worked as an archivist at the German State Archives from 1887-1901.

The goal of scientific history was partially to relay the facts of the past without influence of personal opinion and partially to allow others to come to the same conclusions through the citation of sources. During this period, historians sought to create a history that reflected the unified morals and culture in opposition to a changing contemporary social situation (Appleby, Hunt, & Jacob, 1994, p. 94). The reliance on primary sources for historical writing emphasized the role of archival records as evidence. In scientific history, the archive became the raw material historians used to create their finished work.

In the aftermath of World War I, historians began to question the hegemony of scientific history. Charles Beard and Carl Becker were at the forefront of the movement to question the empirical scientific approach to history. These two historians engaged in historical inquiry through a framework that viewed historical knowledge as relative to the historian and the time in which the history was written (Novick, 1988). Beard and Becker led the relativism movement in historical practice. Historical relativism "is the view that groups from quite different historical epochs will have different modes of thought" (Swoyer, 2003). The relativist movement in historical writing was a conscious step away from the empiricism of Ranke and others and toward a more subjective view of history. In the relativist school of history, interpretation replaced observation. According to Appleby, et al. (1994), this reflected the social and cultural understanding of the times accurately in that changes in American culture created new views of history: "skepticism and relativism about truth, not only in science but also in history and politics, have grown out of the insistent democratization of American society" (p. 3).

Both Beard and Becker wrote from a point of view that stressed the relativity in the relationship between people in the past and their actions. These writings stressed the context of action as much as the result. Examples include Beard's *The Rise of American Civilization* (1927), *America in Midpassage* (1939), and *The American Spirit* (1943), which was coauthored by Mary Beard. In *An Economic Interpretation of the Constitution* (1913), Beard writes an economic history of the United States that focuses on the Founding Fathers' vested economic interest in independence from England. This book was controversial because it was one of the first works of history to claim that the establishment of independence of the United States was not exclusively a moral or metaphysical issue but rather a combination of the two within an economic context. This argument defined relativism within the writing of history in that it posited that the decisions about the founding of the United States were based on relative values rather than single-minded morality. At the time of publication, Beard's point of view broke from traditional historical perspective.

Similarly, Carl Becker wrote controversial relativistic history as well. His collection of four lectures on the Enlightenment, *The Heavenly City of the Eighteenth-Century Philosophers* (1932), focuses on the relationship between Christianity and philosophy in the Age of Reason. In the collection, Becker argues that Christian faith had a large role in the conception of the ideas that would eventually lead to the Enlightenment. Becker also wrote *Everyman His Own Historian* (1935) in which he presents his views on historical relativism. His main arguments in *Everyman* are that historical facts have an inherent subjectivity, that history is a product of historians' imaginations, and contemporary context affects a historian's view of the past.

Both Becker and Beard used relativism as a framework through which they wrote histories that were contrary to much previous scholarly knowledge. Their work was a direct challenge to the notion that history could be written from an objective perspective in which the historian's participation has no effect on the narrative of history. They both argued, sometimes explicitly, for increased subjectivity in historical writing.

In the postwar years, historians were quick to reinforce national unity and show how the Allies were successful in World War II due to their historical destiny. An example of this type of history is Henry Kissinger's (1954) *The World Restored: Metternich, Castlereagh and the Problems of Peace 1812-1822* which focuses on the need for a statesman's morality to be in line with the population he leads in order to lead successfully. While *The World Restored* discusses the history of 19th and early 20th century Europe, its discussion of leaders and their capacity for evil as determined by their own, individual morality is framed by the context of Hitler, the Nazis, and World War II.

Modern methods of gathering historical data created new research opportunities for historians. Consolidation of points of view was helpful during the Cold War in that a unified historical profession could be used for positive propaganda. The influence of World War II propaganda on the writing of history would be relatively short-lived, as varied points of view would develop soon after. An example of these varied points of view are the scholars who founded the Annales School of historical thought.

Between the 1940s and 1960s, the Annales School of historical thought came to prominence in France. Focused around a group of French historians and the journal *Annales d'histoire économique et sociale*, the movement rejected an emphasis on the study of the history of politics, diplomacy and war, which was the focus of many 19th century historians. Instead, the focus of their histories was on "geography, material culture, and what later Annalistes called *mentalités*, or the psychology of the epoch" ("Annales School," 2008). The more well-known historians in the Annales School were Marc Bloch, Lucien Febvre, Georges Duby, and Fernand Braudel. The Annales School and its innovative approach to the content of history opened the field of historical inquiry beyond the history of wars, politics, and governments and began to write the history of people and groups.

During the 1960s and 1970s, more students from varied backgrounds entered universities. The backgrounds of both students and professors became more diverse in universities and, as a result, they questioned the positivist and objective points of view previously supported by so many historians (Appleby, et al., 1994, p. 2). Historians such as Hayden White and Dominick LaCapra argued, based, in part, upon the philosophical writing of poststructuralist Michel Foucault and deconstructionist Jacques Derrida, that the objective truth of scientific history was only one approach for historical inquiry. It is through this sort of questioning that the subfields of social and cultural history were created in order to provide an academically recognized outlet for histories of previously underrepresented groups of people.

If the archival profession has steadily moved to a more autonomous existence in relation to professional historians, what bearing does it have on archival theory? If historiography is the critical summary and explication of the writing of history, it can also be understood to be the discipline in which expectations of the archive are created. Archives are impacted by historiographical paradigms as historians use archival sources differently over time. Understanding the changes in historians' uses of the archive through an examination of changes in historiography illustrates motivations for change in the archive as well. The connection between historiography and archival theory is a close one with each informing the other over time.

The contexts in which archival theory changes are important to further investigation into the creation and development of each archival paradigm. Archival theory has been modified over time through paradigmatic changes and within the influence technology and historiography. At the heart of these shifts in archival appraisal theory over time is the dialectical role the archivist plays in determining what is included in the archive and what is not retained. This dialectic between objective and subjectively created archival appraisal criteria is the theoretical thread that runs through all paradigms and plays a very important role in the changes that occur in each shift. Through tracing the changes in objective and subjective decision-making in archival theory over time, the challenges to existing archival paradigms will be illuminated and elucidated into an intellectual history of archival theory.

3. Consolidation: The Dutch Manual

The basis for most archival theory in North America and beyond is *Handleiding voor het Ordenen en Beschrijven van Archieven*, (*Manual for the Arrangement and Description of Archives*), or the Dutch Manual, as it would come to be known. The Dutch Manual was written by a group of three Dutch archivists: Samuel Muller, Johan A. Feith, and Robert Fruin. It was the product of a consolidation and standardization of much of the practical and localized practices undertaken by archivists in the Netherlands during the 19th century. The Manual was also the impetus for the name of this period in the development of archival theory in that its theoretical basis is one of consolidation and standardization. While the Dutch Manual was written to address issues faced by archivists working at the national level in the Netherlands, the principles it outlines would become and remain important throughout archives worldwide. Concepts like original order (maintaining a *fonds* as it was originally used when the records were active) and respecting records creators as the authoritative voice in terms of record organization were brought together and published in the first widely recognized treatise on archival theory. Many of the concepts archivists take for granted were established in the publication of the Manual.

The Dutch Manual was written in the context of change around the globe, especially in terms of the power and the influence of nations and national governments. Changes in technology and industry dominated the global landscape, which allowed groups of people to move more freely around the world with unprecedented speed. Communication technologies grew with increased use of telephone voice communication. Nations and industries focused their efforts on creating an environment of speed and efficiency. The result of the convergence of these changes was an increased desire for standardization and the spread of the industrial mindset to many areas beyond manufacturing.

Muller, Feith, and Fruin were visionary in their efforts to standardize archival practice in the Netherlands. All three were active, practicing archivists during the time of the Manual's publication, which uniquely qualified them to consolidate and codify their experiences and practices into the first modern archival theory. The publication of the Dutch Manual established the concept that archival theory would begin to change with the rapidly changing world.

Why Consolidate?

The practical and empirical approach to archival activities was based on work that had begun at the beginning of the 19th century with the publication of Josef Anton Oegg's *Ideen einer Theorie der Archivwissenschaft* (*Ideas of a Theory of Archival Science*) in 1804. Oegg's publication sought to be a guide to the "establishment and processing of archives and records" (Ketelaar, 2004). The focus on practical work during this period is, in part, attributed to the fact that European archivists such as Oegg and Muller, Feith, and Fruin were working with one source of records at a time. Whether this source was their local nobility or a newly consolidated government, the focus of collections had been small and singular (Ketelaar, 2004). This narrow focus alleviated the need to place specific archival work in a broader context beyond the goals of consolidation and standardization of practice.

As the national government in the Netherlands began to expand its power and create a national identity, it required a more standardized method of keeping records. The Dutch government, in the persons of Victor de Stuers and Theodoor van Riemsdijk, focused on the consolidation and standardization of archives and archival practices, respectively. Victor de Stuers was head of the Department for Arts and Sciences in the Ministry of the Interior. He has beendescribed as "a strong-minded builder of centralized policy in the field of archives, monuments, and museums" (Barritt, 1993/2003, p. xxxix). Both de Stuers and Theodoor van Reimsdijk, the state archivist of the Netherlands from 1887 to 1912, were concerned with reaching an agreement on the system of classification in state archival repositories (Horsman et al., 2003, pp. xxv & xl). Both men also worked closely with the authors of the Dutch Manual. The goal was to establish semi-standardized national archives that were created using a single methodology. The Dutch Manual was one product of efforts to standardize arrangement and description across archives.

In addition to the Dutch Manual, the middle of the 19th century saw the establishment of archival training centers outside of a university setting that would teach standardized methods of arrangement and description. "This [training] was rather described as passing on experiences than as science. In these cases the necessary capacities on archival sciences and practice had to be acquired during current work or by self-training" (Rumschottel, 2001, pp. 147-148). The training at the new institutions was not enough to create a sense of professional community among 19th century European archivists. What is especially interesting is that the history of the Netherlands, upon which the processes and methodologies in the Dutch Manual are based, was created by the country's role as the crossroads of Europe and was therefore influenced by varied practices and a broad range of approaches.

Dutch archives in the late 19th century were viewed as collections of historical sources and consisted mostly of formal documents, charters, maps, and financial information (Horsman, Ketelaar, & Thomassen, 2003, p. vi). Charters were documents "usually sealed, granting specific rights, setting forth aims and principles, embodying formal agreements, authorizing special privileges or exemptions" (Walne, 1988, p. 75). The records in these archives came from various administrative activities of princes, lords, and city, regional, and state governments. Previous to Muller, Feith, and Fruin's standardization of arrangement and description, Dutch archives were arranged chronologically with little to no regard for *fonds*, a collection of records that originate from the same source. The result were archives that were, in effect, lists of administrative documents and historical resources. For the most part, archivists, who produced ledgers that listed each record in chronological order, provided access to these resources. In smaller archives, the entire text of deeds or charters were reproduced in these registers. As archivists became increasingly responsible for government records, standardization of the description of archival contents became very important. The need for standardization arose only when the contents of archives were compared or consolidated from a few collections into a more centralized archive.

Changes in the Netherlands were a reflection of greater changes in the rest of the world. European countries were hard at work formalizing their colonial relationships in an effort to gain power and land across the globe. Countries like the Netherlands, which had previously been slow to industrialize, attempted to keep pace in other methods of development. The country's system of waterways and reliance on wind power combined with its historical economic position as an economy based upon trade lessened the importance of industrial development in the country in favor of colonization and trade. With its reputation as a liberal center of trade and dependence on economies beyond its borders, the Netherlands constructed, beginning in medieval times, a complex political structure that strove to create consensus in political decisions despite a plethora of competing opinions and interests. This inclusive approach created specialized records and evidence for archivists to preserve and make accessible.

Advances in technology and communication during the last decade of the 19th century were dependent upon empirical science which influenced professional developments of all kinds. Descartes' notions of empiricism and Bacon's scientific method ruled the day in terms of academic study and innovation across disciplines. The study of history during the late 19th century was designated as a second-class academic activity as the telling of the past was not viewed as explicitly scientific in its approach (Novick, 1988). The lack of science in history led historians to seek unity in their practice, to create rules by which peers could judge one another's work. Since scientific laws or theories could not be developed from the history of the world, objectivity was an attempt to substitute peer acceptance for detached hypotheses and results. If historians were unable to scientifically determine, from the evidence at hand, what actions had taken place in the past, the next best approach was to eliminate, as much as possible, historians' own bias in the writing of history. This combination of a desire for scientific results and objective observations led to the reliance on causal relationships, the notion that specific events in history caused specific outcomes.

Professional historians of the late 19th century avoided questioning the philosophic meaning of their work (Appleby, et al., 1994) and instead accepted an objective, scientific orientation as the basis for the writing of history. Rather than question the epistemology of their work, for example, to ask what the relationship between themselves as author and arbiter of knowledge was to the reader, who sought to learn from their work, historians in this period understood their work to be an expression of truth alone. A scientific basis for their work allowed historians to write history with the belief they were relating events from the past as truthfully as possible. The broad acceptance of objectivity through a scientific orientation is equivalent, in the extreme, to Kuhn's (1996/1962) idea that scientists must accept the dominant paradigm in order to complete their work without recreating all knowledge in a specific area. Historians of the late 19th century did not question the philosophical impact or meaning of their work, in part, because they valued unity in historical narrative and believed their work was based only in truth. The belief that their work was based in writing about history "as it happened" helped foster the need for consolidation in the historical profession as well. In a sense, as historians and archivists were essentially the same group of professionals, philosophical blinders were required of professional archivists in favor of practical gains.

Because historians were the primary users of archives, their professional orientation to objective truth created a need for objective records in the archive. Government records became more important than historical church records as national governments consolidated their rule over vast lands. The standardization of archival theory and practice would come to reinforce historians' objective, scientific approach to their own work to mutually benefit archivists and historians alike. One way in which archival theory was created and consolidated during this period was through an emphasis on more standardized practices as revealed in the Dutch Manual. Consolidation of archival practice was necessary to ensure a nationally comparable mode of archival holdings.

The Consolidators

As much as archival theories are a product of the context in which they are created, they are also a product of the theorists themselves. If the Dutch Manual is the basis for contemporary archival theory, then a brief investigation into the biographical history of Dutch archivists will help increase understanding of the context and goals of the Manual's statements. The authors' own professional needs were focused on the relatively small group of archivists in the Netherlands, which are described as being "primarily focused around practical instructions, formulas and such for the creation of inventories" (Horsman et al., 2003, p. xiii).

The three authors of the Dutch Manual were professional archivists who worked closely with historians and professors of history. All three of the Manual's authors were practicing state archivists at the time they wrote and edited the Dutch Manual and therefore very familiar with the needs of large government entities. The authors were well-versed in the difficulties and issues faced by contemporary Dutch archivists. Johan Feith was the state archivist of Groningen. He provided text for 26 of the 99 sections in the Manual, though was criticized for having a laconic writing style that differed greatly from that of the other two authors (Horsman et al., 2003). Feith was the first of the authors to die, doing so in 1913.

Robert Fruin worked as the state archivist of Zeeland and worked with government records and archives. He wrote the archival manual for the national government of the Netherlands (van Bath, 1948, p. 236 & 257). After his co-authorship of the Manual, he published another manual that focused on legal work, which was a popular point of emphasis at the time of its publication in 1922.

Samuel Muller was perhaps the most well-known of the three authors. Muller's predominant experience was as a state archivist with a background in government records. His preference was that the Manual focus on the importance of official records (Horsman, et al., 1898/2003), and not necessarily discuss personal records or manuscripts. In fact, his work focused on inventories of the records of the bishops and city of Utrecht who were, from 1000 to 1300, two of the most important power centers in the northern Netherlands. Muller supported non-critical historical research that focused on the study of diplomatics and paleography in the interest of establishing authenticity in records. Muller continued his archival work until his death in 1922.

The Manual and Its Theory

The epistemological boundaries of the Manual are, for the most part, focused on creating practical unity, prescription of methods, and delineation of specific instructions to archivists. The focus on the standardization of practices allowed the authors to avoid more philosophical and theoretical questions of objectivity in their new conception of the archive. However, in more than one instance, the authors do engage in some theorizing and influence future concepts of the archive with specific comments such as "This section contains a wish rather than a fixed rule" (Muller, Feith, & Fruin, 1898/2003, p. 46). In fact, the Dutch Manual sought to use the consolidated national archives of the Netherlands as a case study from which to extrapolate archival methods and theory. The authors were successful in this attempt.

Contemporary interpretations of the Manual have neglected to take into account the unique political and governmental history that has so highly influenced archival practice and the creation of rules from specific instances. Muller et al. are aware of this, though they seek to create "modern archival doctrine" without caveats that could undermine unity in theory and approach to archives. The publication of the manual was "aimed at the standardization of professional practice," and was forcefully implemented by Dutch archivists. A lack of codified professional training for archivists and a desire to create standardized archives created a need for normalization and regulation among archivists of the time. The Dutch Manual was the vehicle through which these paradigmatic goals were sought. Muller, Feith, and Fruin claim that localization of practice is not discouraged but their intention is clearly to standardize practices and subsequently encourage local deviation, in that order.

The authors of the Dutch Manual promote the notion that each archival collection is composed of unique records of historical value so that any attempt at standardization of practice is tempered by the needs of the archival collection itself. By allowing for both centralized and localized practice, the Manual can remain focused on practical matters such as description and arrangement. In the Manual, the archive is described as a living organism that changes with the organization's function. Therefore, the Manual's purpose is to guide individualized practice through principles of archival work. Muller et al. stop short of naming this a unified archival theory, but the principles in the Dutch Manual indeed have functioned in this manner. Though there really is no control in regards to how individual archives acquire specialized practices, a unified archival theory creates a tension between standardization and uniqueness, between normalization and local variations and, ultimately, between objectivity and subjectivity.

The release of these tensions is the establishment of a scientific approach to archival theory. The Dutch Manual seeks to employ such an approach to overcome the tensions between unique collections and standardization. The bulk of the text explicates strategies of description and arrangement. Muller et al. (1898/2003) focus on specific details, such as the form of dates and highly specific definitions of document types such as *vidimus*[1] and *transumpt*[2] (p. 208 & 214). These types of specific definitions are indeed important to the epistemological basis and viability of the standardization in the Dutch Manual. Highly specific definitions of minute portions of archival work serve to both standardize theoretical terms and create a unified basis from which a scientific archival practice can be created. Muller, Feith, and Fruin were highly successful in their attempt to establish scientific principles in archival theory. Indeed, Theodore Schellenberg, an influential archival theorist himself, hailed the Dutch Manual as the starting point for archival science and administration (Ketelaar, 2004).

Though scientific archival theory has its own set of epistemological complexities, its use can create another tension between the internal (archival) and external (parent organization). Muller, et al. describe the archive as being "closely bound up with the sphere of activity of the administrative body or of the official to whom it owes its origin" (p. 127). These tensions can add further impediments to a complete expression of archival theory in practice. For the most part, the Manual avoids this tension by virtue of its focus on the practicalities of the consolidation and standardization of arrangement and description practices.

The theories put forth in the Dutch Manual are a consolidation of archival theory from medieval times to the

---

[1] A vidimus is defined in The Dutch Manual (p. 208) as: "a formal document in which a sovereign or other person clothed with authority gives a transcript of another formal document for the purpose of confirming it, or one in which a person authorized to attest documents gives a transcript worth of general credit of another formal document," (Italics in original).
[2] A transumpt is defined in the Dutch Manual (p. 208) as: "*an authenticated copy of a formal document,*" (Italics in original).

beginning of the 20th century. The concepts within it are an amalgamation of ideas from past practice and desired futures. The English translation of the Dutch word *archief* is one example of the transformative force of professional folkways and illustrates the importance of interpretation in the development of archival theory. Upward (1998) notes that the concept of *archief* is translated, in English, to mean an archival collection. In Dutch, the meaning is much more specific and centered upon everything in a collection officially received or produced by an administrative body that was intended to remain in the custody of that body.

The Manual defines the archive as: "the whole of the written documents, drawings and printed matter, officially received or produced by an administrative body or one of its officials, in so far as these documents were intended to remain in the custody of that body or of that official," (Muller et al., p. 13). It is clear that the emphasis is on the collection, the "organic" whole of records from the creators. Part of this reasoning is the term "officially" in the definition above which refers to official documents as the point of emphasis for a collection. If the records were produced by an authoritative body like a government or church it would be difficult, if not impossible, to discard a document that contained unofficial information, since the concept of the document in this context is already granted privileged status. In effect, the Dutch Manual allows records creators to appraise their own records since it is unlikely that non-official records would be transferred to the archive during this time.

Though many of the concepts involved in the creation of an archive may be present in the archive as a whole, the Dutch definition is narrow and supplies highly stringent criteria for records. Upward (1998) calls attention to the discrepancy between this definition and contemporary colloquialism: "An archive in the Dutch definition is a creation built up in the conduct of business, not a collection, as most people understand the term" (¶ 23). Explicit appraisal theory is absent from the Manual because the issue could be avoided altogether. The definition of the archive limits the types of records that can be included. The Manual also avoids appraisal and the dialectic between objectivity and subjectivity through a focus on more practical matters like arrangement and description.

The main theoretical reason for the very specific definition of the archive for Muller et al. is the narrow definition of the record itself. They note that the archive should consist of specific types of records. Muller et al. (1898/2003) define these records as formal documents: "Formal documents are written documents drawn up in the appropriate form, so that they may serve as evidence of what is mentioned in them" (p. 206). Further discussion of the contents of the archive includes maps, but not objects, which are best kept at museums. A translator's note says that photographs would be included if the Manual were written at a later date (Leavitt, 1898/2003). The concept of naturalness of the archive is created if the contents of the archive are tightly controlled by specific record type. This necessitates an expansive knowledge of the archives' contents. Harris (2004) notes that Muller et al. define a record as a piece of information that should not be questioned and is self-explanatory.

The bulk of the Manual's text is dedicated to discussions of practice in terms of arrangement and description. The focus of the arrangement portion is on definition and delineation of *fonds*. Horsman et al. (2003) note that this is indeed a large contribution to archival arrangement: "The pioneering work of the *Manual* lies in defining the archival *fonds*; in the formulation of the connection between the archive and the function of those who create it" (p. xvi). While the Dutch Manual solidified the use of the concept of *respect des fonds* in archival practice, Barritt (1993) and Moore (2008) note that the principle was in place well before publication of Muller, Feith, and Fruin's work. The principle, which is based upon the idea that records creators' and users' context for the arrangement of their own records should be represented in the archive, is a simple one: use the system used to create the records to keep the records arranged. This principle also extends to archival collections that should be kept complete rather than separated by subject or changed as organizations and entities disband or change function (Muller et al. 1898/2003).

Arrangement is indeed the archival concept that commands the most discussion and theoretical discourse in the Dutch Manual. Muller, Feith, and Fruin based their theory of arrangement on the combination of two archival concepts: *provenienzprinzip* and *registraturprinzip*. The former is the establishment of the importance of the imposition of the records' internal structure upon them as a result of recordkeeping processes based upon the activities the organization undertook to create the records (Upward, 1998). The latter is a method of records control applied to the records of the organization's registry, the list of records held by the organization. In this case, the classification scheme is based on the same scheme the organization used to create the registry. These two concepts existed independently of one another prior to the publication of the Dutch Manual. The Manual brought the two practices together to create a new concept of provenance that included both lists: the former created by the records, the latter created by the organization of those records in lists or registries. The concept included the requirement that the archivist study the organization that created the records in order to better understand how the records should be arranged. This study would produce a framework for the arrangement of records, regardless of format. The third view of archival provenance is that the organization of the records should correspond to the organization that created the records. Provenance is the concept used to help guide the archivist in the creation of series, or groups of records created by the same department within an organization. The main series of an organization's archive is considered to be the backbone of the subsidiary series in the collection.

The archivist is given even more freedom in terms of arrangement in that Muller, Feith, and Fruin allow for the main series of records to be subdivided in any way the archivist may see fit. For instance, the subdivisions of a series do not need to reflect the subdivisions of the administrative body (Muller et al., p. 89). Subject-oriented subdivisions are also permissible. This type of freedom allows the archivist to arrange and rearrange records in order to best represent the collection as a whole. It also allows one to take preservation and storage into consideration. In terms of theory, this principle illustrates the tension between the philosophical ideal of objective archives at the intersection of the reality of subjectivity in archival practice. By giving the power of rearrangement to the archivist, this theoretical construct allows the archivist to determine how the archive is perceived and used.

Muller, Feith, and Fruin encourage archivists to make subjective decisions in terms of arrangement. The Dutch Manual notes: "The point of view according to which an archival collection is to be arranged must be left to the judgment of the archivist, who has to take into account in this matter the nature of the collection" (p. 142). The increase in the tension between objectivity in theory and subjectivity in practice is great in this situation as the archivist may be interested in commanding more power over their collections rather than following objective principles of the profession over time. However, given the contexts in which the archivists were working, the commitment to this theoretical point of view is somewhat ambivalent. The Dutch Manual states: "But ... each archival collection demands its own arrangement and, however desirable it may be that general rules be established for this, one should refrain from giving directions about it" (Muller et al., p. 142). The unique information contained in the archive is of little value if it is arranged in such a manner that it is not useful to users, both casual and experienced. The discussion of arrangement in the Dutch Manual is a historically important step toward stating and consolidating various practices employed over time.

Along with arrangement, the Dutch Manual is devoted to explicating Muller, Feith, and Fruin's notions of description of archival material. One of the most influential theoretical postulations made in the Dutch Manual regarding description is that individual items should not be described since to do so would deprecate the integrity of the whole collection. This point of view is critical toward understanding the solidification of the view of the archival collection as an entire collection rather than a group of related records or even a collection of documents. Muller et al. set the standard for the understanding of many aspects of archival theory through their conception of the archive as a discreet and whole entity that should remain unbroken.

Description is not immune to the tension between objective theory and subjective practice in the Manual. The split between objective and subjective approaches to description activities is evidenced in the directions given in the Manual regarding the creation of calendars and inventories. Calendars are chronologically arranged tables of content of all formal documents in the collection. Inventories are lists of series and records that reflect the contents of the archive and can be understood to be the most objective representation of the archive. The use of calendars changes the context of their creation: "Here the interest of the present-day searcher alone is most important. One does not ask what interest the corporate body in whose collection the document is found had in the document, but what interest history may have in it" (Muller et al. 1898/2003, p. 165). The best practice is described as writing calendars from the point of view of the archival collection, not the archivist. The focus shifts from objective representation of action taken to subjective possible future uses. Calendars should be written from a distinctly different point of view than the records themselves are arranged.

The Terms Are Established

Though the theory in the Dutch Manual is constructed from a somewhat oblique angle, it nonetheless defines the epistemological orientation of almost all subsequent archival theory. It is important to explore, then, the gaps in the theory presented in the Dutch Manual to understand the theoretical shortcomings subsequent archivists found necessary to fill and change with their own theories. The Manual attempted to consolidate many archival theories into one in the Netherlands thereby working against the subjectivity of individual archivists. One such case is the Manual's definition of the concept of the record. The concept of the record in the Dutch Manual, like the definition of the archive itself, is one of naturalness, one that is organic in nature, and unquestionably objective (Harris, 2004). In terms of records, the Dutch Manual is also dedicated to the organization of various types of records and how they should be handled based on an epistemologyhat highly values objectivity. What is interesting is that the authors of the Dutch Manual allow the archivist a wide theoretical berth when describing how archivists should deal with well-defined records, especially in terms of arrangement. This stems, in part, from the uniqueness of the contents of each archival collection, but also because archivists are indeed human and interested in influencing the outcome of their work, even if that would require being less objective in their approach.

The process through which minutes become part of the archive illustrates Muller, Feith, and Fruin's understanding that not all potential records are of equal value. In this case, the authors note that the approved minutes are the important records for the archive and that the draft, including rough drafts, memoranda, or the corrected drafts, have no meaning after the adopted minutes exist (Muller et al.). While this is indeed the case from an official, strictly evidentiary perspective, it does place a hierarchy of value on records to make some (rough drafts, memoranda, etc.) less valuable than others. This may seem like a minor detail in the larger scheme of the theories in the Manual, but it is an important aspect in understanding the tension between objectivity and subjectivity in archival theory. Once the valuation of records exists, one cannot guarantee completely objective results. It is this kernel of humanism, of subjective allowance in the Dutch Manual, that portends a difficult theoretical path in the future on which archivists will contentiously travel with an undetermined end.

Rumschottel (2001) argues that during the first third of the 19th century, archivists were already well down this path and had to deal with an increase in the amount of records coming into the archive. With the bulk of records on the rise, archivists needed to find a way to more efficiently categorize their holdings. Instead of subject classification, which Muller et al. argue against very strongly, archivists began to place more value on context and provenance in order to help them deal with increased demands on their time. One of the best examples is the continuance of the notion of *respect des fonds*, or the principle of provenance. The notion that the records created by discreet groups within organizations should remain together in the archive was established in the 1840s in France (Moore, 2008). *Respect des fonds* itself is a product of subjective theoretical orientation in that it has been inducted into the implicit theory of the Dutch Manual. While the arrangement and description of material by *fonds* may seem like second nature to contemporary archivists, there was a time when, as a profession, archivists shifted paradigms and agreed to a theory that valued new and different types of information about records.

The records archivists of the late 19th century based their work upon were, for the most part, medieval. These medieval and government records were part of the respective archives because of previous mandates, whether historical or governmental. The concept of the relative valuing records, especially since there were relatively small numbers of them, may have been unnecessary during the formulation of concepts for the Dutch Manual. Alternatively, perhaps the definition of the archive was such that the exclusion of some records would have lessened the amount of objectivity in the work of the archivist. Regardless, it was very important for Dutch archivists to adhere to an objective, scientific approach to archival theory in order to be taken seriously by historians and remain viable to fellow archivists as well. The Dutch Manual was their guide in the creation of consolidated Dutch archives.

The Manual's Critics

It is fairly easy to criticize the epistemological approach of the Dutch Manual from a historical vantage point, to give examples of the misinterpretation and mischaracterization of its methodologies as prescriptive and rigid theories. Another point of view is that the practical approach and rigidity found in the Manual's theory was the point of unification that contributed to a new, consolidated archival paradigm. The Dutch Manual can be understood as the fulcrum that helped transform archival methodologies into a single methodology, especially for arrangement and description. The Dutch Manual is a specialized set of rules conceived around the needs of state archivists in the Netherlands as they began to create large, national archives out of smaller, local, and non-standard collections of predominantly medieval records. In order to create properly functioning national archives, standard practices were required. New types of national records were being created that needed to be archived and made accessible across the country. The Dutch Manual helped this process work well for the Netherlands and for other countries as they began to participate in similar consolidations, using the Manual as a professional guide. The issues and criticism of the text began when European archivists were faced with new problems leading up to and after World War I. The issues were numerous and included the archives of temporary governmental agencies, the increased communication and record generation of war, and the destruction of land, infrastructure, and death that occurred during war. These changes created a crisis in archival theory. Where the theory present in the Dutch Manual focuses on arrangement and description of defined records, it falls short when the cultural mandate or archival context changes. After World War I, the focus of archival theory changed from an internal to external perspective, from old to new, and multiple ages of records.

With the Foundation Laid

For Muller, Feith, and Fruin, maintaining the theoretical status quo was a difficult proposition at best. Publication in archival science during the 18th and 19th centuries reflected the continuing shift of historical use as well as juridical uses of the archive. This was also reflected in the needs of historians, the primary users of archives, who sought official records and evidence of action.

The Dutch Manual is the consolidation of Continental European archival theory as expressed through practices begun during medieval times on medieval records. The authors were able to create an archival theory without the need to answer explicit questions of objectivity and subjectivity through a focus on standard arrangement and description practices. This served to ensure that local archival holdings could be easily consolidated with and compared to relatively new national archives. The consolidation of archives was part of a larger political movement to create a more cohesive nation in the Netherlands, the basis of which was its archival holdings from the past.

Written during a time in which a scientific approach was the ideal for both archivists and historians, the "rules" contained in the Manual strive to be objective and directive. While they were able to create refined archival practices, Muller, Feith, and Fruin were also successful in creating a tension between objectively derived prescription and subjective practice. Their system worked well for Dutch archives that consisted of medieval records and contemporary government documents. The Dutch system continued to be influential in archival theory beyond the end of the 19th century. It would take the total war of World War I to make archivists reevaluate the theoretical and practical emphasis placed on arrangement and description. As new government agencies and temporary war-related entities were created and disbanded, archivists were faced with new challenges. These challenges were met by Sir Hilary Jenkinson's theories.

4. Confirmation and Reinforcement: Sir Hilary Jenkinson's *A Manual of Archive Administration*

Sir Hilary Jenkinson is one of the most well-known archival theorists and one whose work has had an immense impact upon archival theory. Jenkinson's *A Manual of Archive Administration*, published in 1922 and revised in 1937, is one of the most widely recognized treatises on the theory of archives and archival work. Though the Manual contains many practical guidelines and several appendices that focus on practice, Jenkinson's work is, for the most part, devoted to the moral and theoretical reasons for keeping archives. Jenkinson's Manual is indeed one of the first comprehensive statements of archival theory, one that explicitly separates theory from practice, and makes recommendations regarding a theoretical approach to archives.

In his Manual, Jenkinson constructs a theory of archives that builds upon core concepts from The Dutch Manual, including original order and provenance. Jenkinson defines archives in a more restrictive manner than do Muller, Feith, and Fruin, which necessitates a new definition of the concept of the record. These new definitions are placed in a theory that actively seeks to avoid the question of appraisal through a proposal that records' creators cull documents and records before they enter the archive. The result is that Jenkinson's legacy has been defined as one of custody, both in terms of unbroken lines of ownership and a specific custodial, "keeper" role for archivists.

Jenkinson is characterized as remaining steadfastly opposed, both theoretically and practically, to the archivist who seeks to make appraisal part of their professional work. Because Jenkinson's theory of the archive is dependent upon unbroken custody, the maintenance of the evidentiary nature of records, and, perhaps most importantly, the context which surrounds each individual record, the destruction of any record is illogical. Jenkinson creates an archival theory based upon the notion that the type of information held in archives should be similar to if not reflect the type of information kept in medieval archives and other archives of the past. Jenkinson does allow the archivist an increased amount of power in terms of carrying out his duties, but constructs strict limits at the edges of the definitions. As in the Dutch Manual, this subjectivity operates within the restrictions of truth, progress, and the infallibility of human law. The dialectic between objectivity and subjectivity in archival theory, in Jenkinson's view, is virtually non-existent or should be dispensed with altogether as unproductive. Through the reinforcement of objective archival theory, Jenkinson's theory values objectivity over all other approaches.

Reinforcement in the Face of Change

Globally, the 1920s was a decade shaped by World War I. The first "total war" that included nearly every country in Europe and countries on other continents wrought physical destruction on its cities and cultural chaos on most Europeans. Technological innovations in fighting ushered in a new era of technological change across the globe. Many social and cultural changes occurred as a result of the war and its effects on Europeans, including the rebuilding of cities and governments after large-scale destruction.

Combat technology motivated an acceleration in terms of scientific and industrial innovation. Fixed-wing airplanes and tanks were used for the first time in battle. Submarines and wireless communication also played a large role in the conflict. Changes in civilian uses of technology also took place. The ability to transfer information quickly over long distances without text via the telephone shrank the importance of geographical location in terms of communication. Writing was also drastically changed by the increased use of the typewriter. The mechanical reproduction of text and information increased the number of records produced daily as typists were able to create many copies of documents quickly and accurately. Innovation in communications technology would lead to important changes in value of the written word and use of archival records.

While World War I signaled the end of the Ottoman Empire, it also began the sunset of the British Empire. The result of the fall of the Ottoman Empire was the last major expansion of Britain as a colonial power, which led to a new British presence in Palestine, Iraq, South-West Africa, and parts of Germany. Expansion came to an end relatively quickly with the succession of individual British Dominions beginning with Canada in 1923. Former colonial holdings would follow suit, with Australia the last Dominion to enter into a treaty independently in 1940.

Along with changes in land holdings and the relationship to its subjects, the ways and means of British government and its subjects underwent important and rapid change during this time as well. Beginning in 1918, the right to vote was expanded with the Representation of the People Act which extended the franchise to woman voters, though equal suffrage was not achieved until 1928. In 1919, the Housing Act created new opportunities for people across class lines to own their own homes and begin to leave inner-city life. The voting population in Britain was eager to participate in the rapid political changes that took place and, in 1922, elected the Labour Party's first majority in national government. With changes in citizenship came new expectations of government and record keeping. New roles for government included accountability to citizens as well as expanded rights and expectations of the guarantee that those rights would be available in the form of government records.

As with technological change, the war proved to be a watershed moment in many Briton's lives. A growing lack of trust in the government was in contrast to the faith that Britain was on a righteous path before World War I. Leventhal (1995) notes: "Pre-First World War Whig orthodoxy involved a belief in the progressive quality of British political history characterized by the steady advance of orderly parliamentary democracy under responsible leadership" (p. 362). The results of World War I were devastating to this faith in the British government. Though the Entente was victorious in the war, the social and psychological costs were enormous: "After the upheaval of the First World War, this orthodoxy came under attack from both the Left and the Right as the optimism on which it had rested evaporated in the face of experience" (Leventhal, p. 362). The combination of new expectations and a suspicion of the government created a difficult position for British citizens and archivists after the war.

The disparity between the end of the war, a cause for celebration; and the expansive and quick technological, cultural, and governmental changes, a possible cause for concern or bewilderment, was not felt among British historians. While past ideologies, including an absolute value in objectivity in the writing of history, were being questioned by popular media and citizens, many British historians remained steadfastly attached to objectivity in their work (Leventhal, 1995). Many British historians of the time focused their studies on medieval and local history, which are less subject to contemporary popular movements and an illustration of the cultural reinforcements that took place after the war. Viewed in this light, these historians' commitment to objectivity in their work becomes less stubborn and more sympathetic as an attempt to create at least a semblance of order out of chaos.

Immediately before and even during World War I, British historians were involved with the writing of local history. In fact, this was the main movement that would spawn the foundation of county record societies, the earliest of which were in Lincolnshire, in 1910, and Northamptonshire, in 1920 (Cannon, 1997, p. 588). Local historians and record societies were typically interested in their immediate geographic surroundings which was reflected in their writing and collections. The situation is somewhat similar to that described by Muller, Feith, and Fruin in the Dutch Manual in which small organizations create idiosyncratic collections and local historians write about them without attempting to connect narrowly focused local histories to larger historical trends. The Church of England and its clergy were also very involved in county record societies due to the interest in medieval buildings and churches. As a result, many of the records held in county record societies were from medieval times. During the 1920s and 1930s, county record societies increasingly hired professional archivists, who for the most part, were also trained historians (Cannon, 1997). While the historians who most frequently used county record societies remained amateurs, the archival profession was beginning to take shape in Britain with national archivists like Jenkinson in the vanguard of professionalization.

Local history was perhaps the most popular mode of history during the early 20th century in Britain, though social and military histories were also of interest to historians. Social historians of early 20th century Britain had been highly influenced by the Scottish Enlightenment. Important thinkers of the Scottish Enlightenment include David Hume, one of the originators of the concepts that would become the scientific method, and Adam Smith, author of

The Wealth of Nations, the first treatise on economics. The influence of positivity and progress, the notions that, together, posit that humanity is on a cumulatively upward journey toward perfection, or enlightenment, was present in British histories like those written by George Trevelyan and Frederick Maitland. The former author was proud of his subjective historical disposition, yet maintained positivity in *Lord Grey of the Reform Bill* (1920) and *England Under Queen Anne* (1930-34). With the exception of Trevelyan, historical writing before World War I took an overall empirical approach to the gathering and analysis of historical facts. The combination of positivity and empiricism created a British history that relied upon a scientific approach and created cumulatively positive views of Britain's past.

In contrast, military history was viewed as amateurish and unworthy of serious academic inquiry. Before World War I, military history in Britain was the history of far-off wars fought to enlarge or maintain empire, not domestic history (Cannon, 1997). For the most part, military history relied on straightforward narrative rather than any revealing insights, which most likely contributed to a limited circulation and interest. Very soon after World War I, however, interest in British military history would increase, in part because of the work of Sir Hilary Jenkinson and his work on the archives of World War I.

The history of pre-World War I British archives is fairly linear. Many of the most important documents held in these archives were from the medieval period and included the Domesday Book, the Magna Carta, and Edward VIII's abdication letter from the 20th century as well as other, lesser-known documents. Nobles' wills were kept separately in Somerset House in London while the parliamentary archives were the purview of the House of Lords record office in Westminster (Cannon, 1997). The General Registry Office held material that would be considered archival within almost any paradigm. These records included social information like births, deaths, and marriages from 1837 on through Jenkinson's time. Much like the archives in the Netherlands before the writing of the Dutch Manual, British archives in the 1920s were not standardized. Discrepancies abounded between type of archival institution and the type of records they held by location. In order for any standardization or possible uniform organization to take place, British archivists working in this paradigm needed to reinforce their theoretical approach to archives before they could standardize their holdings and physical archives. One of the first theoretical steps toward this reinforcement was to hold objectivity in archival work in high esteem.

The first practical step toward standardization was the creation of County Record Offices. The office in Bedfordshire claims to be the oldest archives department and was established in 1913. The publication of Jenkinson's Manual would inspire new County Record Offices to open with nine new locations between 1920 and 1939 (Cannon, 1997). In his Manual, Jenkinson precisely describes and defines archives, records, and the role of the archivist, all in an effort to begin to establish an independent archival profession within a newly conceived and developed national archival system in Britain.

Jenkinson's Career

Hilary Jenkinson was born on November 1, 1882, in south London, the son of a real estate agent father. Jenkinson graduated with first class honors from Cambridge with a degree in classics. Two years later, he took a post at the Public Records Office in London. He would work in that government department for the next 48 years. Jenkinson was not content to be a career bureaucrat in the service of government and sought opportunities to engage in archival work through a variety of professional means. These means included teaching classes in paleography and archives at the School of Librarianship at University College, London from 1920 to 1925 and diplomatics and archives at King's College London from 1920 to 1947 (Eastwood, 2002).

By the time Jenkinson began to rise in the ranks of the Public Records Office, the previous practice of appointments through favors and patronage was in decline. Working as an archivist was slowly becoming a viable profession reliant upon qualifications and training. Jenkinson was one of the first modern British archivists to hold the position as it became a viable profession. As a result, Jenkinson was very active in fledgling professional organizations. He was instrumental in forming the British Records Association, which began operation in 1932. Jenkinson also was one of the leaders in founding the International Council on Archives after World War II.

While working at the British Public Records Office, Jenkinson received a commission from the Carnegie Endowment for International Peace to develop methods to preserve war records (Eastwood, 2002). The result of his work is the *A Manual of Archive Administration*. While the records of World War I far surpassed any previous notions of record bulk, they were also the result of national and technological change. Even during Jenkinson's tenure at the Records Office, the means of mechanical reproduction had an immense impact upon archivists' work. Jenkinson was tasked, in part, with bringing archival practice into the modern world while under pressure from government and military supervisors to work with speed and within budgetary constraints.

The focus of Jenkinson's Manual is war archives, an archival situation which exacerbates all the usual difficulties of selection, arrangement, description, and preservation due to the often temporary nature of military and government configurations during war time. The war archives Jenkinson worked with included documentation of strategy, equipment, and the experiences of those who fought, but were quickly disregarded after Britain's successful completion of fighting. The situation in which Jenkinson found British archives was different than any previous archival context, especially the types of archives described in the Dutch Manual. While the Dutch Manual emphasized arrangement and description, it was written from a point of view that relied upon time for a slow accumulation of archival material. Jenkinson had relatively little time to preserve Britain's national experience in World War I. As a result, he would develop a new archival paradigm out of this professional crisis to fill the gaps between the previous paradigm and his professional needs. The result would eventually be adopted as a viable archival theory, one that reinforced many of the previously consolidated archival concepts in the Dutch Manual.

Jenkinson's Manual is the first English language work of archival theory to be published and read widely. While many of the theoretical constructs originate in Muller, Feith, and Fruin's work, Jenkinson improves upon their basic practical guidelines with further explanation, and delineation of boundaries and suggestions. The most comprehensive and perhaps unique aspect of Jenkinson's theory is the definition of records and archives, which, in its strength and absolutism, is a distinguishing feature of Jenkinson's work. In Jenkinson's terms the definition of the archive and its records become a catalyst that would transform British archival work from low-level bureaucratic work to a fully functional, intellectually rigorous endeavor fully capable of archiving large amounts of records in a time-sensitive manner.

Jenkinson's Steadfast Archives

The reinforcement of Muller, Feith, and Fruin's work is apparent throughout Jenkinson's Manual. The broad and comprehensive statements on archival theory restate and expand upon Muller, Feith, and Fruin's work, especially in terms of arrangement. Jenkinson cites Muller, Feith, and Fruin liberally throughout the arrangement section of his Manual. The shared approach to arrangement is logical as both works base their approaches on records and experiences with medieval European archives. Different archivists held these archives for quite a long time, and, as such, the archives experienced some significant difficulties such as inconsistency and shortsightedness (Jenkinson, 1922).

Archives of the past are not the only concern of the Manual. Jenkinson proposes lofty goals for war archives, the archives with which he is most concerned, which include "the preservation of the completest possible record of war effort as shown in the written remains of every kind of Local and Public Administration, with no thought for sectional and secondary interests until that first object is accomplished" (Jenkinson, 1922, p. 166). Jenkinson seeks to capitalize on the impulse toward national archival consolidation which began in the late 1910s and early 1920s in Britain. His proposition was difficult, though, since his specific goal was to retain a complete record of the history of war. In order to reach that goal, Jenkinson was forced to deal with the unique situation created by war with its temporary organizations, lack of funding for historical purposes, and possible destruction of records due to fighting.

Open to new answers to new problems, Jenkinson recommends that the records' creators who were active during the war return to their posts to cull records before they enter the archive (Jenkinson, 1922). Jenkinson also proposes that archival institutions cooperate with one another across political boundaries to create archives that reflect Britain's national character in regards to World War I. Here, Jenkinson's goal is to create a complete archive of a single moment in time. His theoretical point of view is to save all that is possible to save and begin to determine how to make the material useful after the fact. The time pressure Jenkinson faced was immense. If war records were not preserved quickly and soon after the end of the war, their context and availability would be severely compromised.

Jenkinson understood past paradigms to be lacking in theoretical orientation regarding the specific issues found in the creation of war archives. He was not satisfied with the specific rules and detailed instructions found in the Dutch Manual, for instance. For one, the Dutch Manual was very specific to the archival needs of the Netherlands. British government and history had very different archival needs. While both countries created new archival paradigms during a period of archival consolidation, each geographical context remained unique. Jenkinson was faced with unprecedented amounts of unorganized records from various levels of government from local to national, including the military. Jenkinson and British archivists experienced Kuhn's crisis, in which professionals suddenly realize their professional response to a problem—in this case the creation of the archives of World War I—cannot be satisfactorily made with the current theories at hand. A new theory was required.

Jenkinson builds on the concepts in the Dutch Manual, but differs in some significant ways as well. The terms of Jenkinson's work are broad-based theoretical statements where Muller, Feith, and Fruin discuss the practical matters of keeping archives. Theoretically, Jenkinson's goals are different than those of the Dutch Manual. Tschan notes that Jenkinson goal is "to come to some fundamental understanding of archival principles that could, in turn, guide the creation of the archives of the present and the future" (Tschan, 2002, p. 177-8). This goal is indeed accomplished, but the result is based upon the records and types of information from both Jenkinson's and the archival past. Unfortunately for Jenkinson, his theory, based on well-known archives of the past, was published just as massive, inconceivable changes in technology and culture were on the horizon. Jenkinson's reliance on medieval record structures would also probably account for at least a portion of his theoretical disagreements with Schellenberg and some of the basic ideas of North American appraisal theory.

The most basic theoretical aspect of Jenkinson's work is that his definition of archives is that they are a substitute for memory. As such, Jenkinson's definition of the archive begins as an artificial memory, paper replacements for memorization and oral transmission of evidence. For Jenkinson, the emphasis has changed from the Dutch Manual in that the goal of his Manual is the professional reinforcement of archival concepts rather than exclusively the consolidation of disparate ideas into a coherent whole. The result is that the concepts in the Dutch Manual are reinforced by Jenkinson's own ideas, which result in the creation of a new and distinct archival paradigm.

One aspect by which Jenkinson's theory differentiates itself from the Dutch Manual is the treatment of public and private archives as one archival corpus. Theoretically, this is an example of the convergence of public, legal, and private memories which would become more complete nearly 70 years later in the United States. Jenkinson (1922) defines all archives with the following criteria:

1. Archives are accumulations of records, not collections brought together after the fact.
2. Archives are not normally drawn up for the information of posterity.

3. The fact and nature of Custody are all-important for Archives.
4. Archives were an actual part of Administration and in use during the course of the administration's business.
5. Archives are interrelated and depend on context for their meaning.

Jenkinson stresses that within the defined archive it is of the utmost importance that records that were created together "*...the Archives resulting from the work of an Administration which was an organic whole, complete in itself, capable of dealing independently, without any added or external authority, with every side of any business which could normally be presented to it*" (italics in original) (Jenkinson, 1922, p. 84).

Indeed, the concept of the record is central to Jenkinson's archival theory. Tschan (2002) notes that, in Jenkinson's definition, the difference between the archive and records is marginal, if it exists at all: "For Jenkinson, there is no such definitive and transformative point at which records become archives ... Jenkinson considered records and archives synonymous" (p. 18). This lack of a distinction in Jenkinson's theory is vital to understanding his theoretical terms such as a "natural accumulation of records" and the disavowal of archivists interfering with original order and *fonds* in the form of appraisal. Jenkinson himself defines archives throughout his Manual variously as, "*... documents which formed part of an official transaction and were preserved for official reference,*" and "*both documents specially made for, and documents included in an official transaction*" (Italics in original) (Jenkinson, 1922, pp. 4 & 5). Archival documents, meanwhile, are defined as having been:

> *... drawn up or used in the course of an administrative or executive transaction (whether public or private) of which itself formed a part; and subsequently preserved in their own custody for their own*

information by the person or persons responsible for that transaction and their legitimate successors. (Italics in original) (Jenkinson, 1922, p. 11)

These are strict definitions that allow relatively few documents the privilege of being qualified as archives. Jenkinson bases the evidentiary nature of archives on the notion that the records kept in archives are indeed evidence because they comprise "the facts of the case" (Jenkinson, 1922, p. 4). Indeed, if each record retained in an archive had honestly been evaluated closely and thoroughly as Jenkinson proposes, the evidentiary nature of any single document in an archive would be unquestionable. The need to appraise records would also be negligible as well. These stringent criteria were likely to allow archivists to avoid explicit appraisal decisions in favor of rejecting possible material for the archive on the basis of custody or lack of original order.

Jenkinson defines three basic types of records which comprise all archival material: material that was received by an office, material created for external audiences, and material created for internal audiences. These categories map directly to what Jenkinson later refers to as "received, issued, and proceedings" (1922, p. 23 & 31). If archivists and records creators can conceive of their work in such a manner, the preservation of official custody, a condition Jenkinson requires for archives, will ensure the proper creation of archives of a manageable size without the execution of any appraisal activities. Further qualification for archives resides in the accumulation, not the collection of records. Jenkinson describes the accumulation of records as they become inactive as a natural, organic process.

Another condition for archives is the motivation for the creation of records which can become archives. Jenkinson states that records must be created without historical uses in mind, that the creation of records is done to carry out business at hand at the time the record is created. Though the information contained in the records will become valuable for varied and completely different uses than originally intended, there should be no acknowledgment of the possibility of historical value at the point of record creation (Jenkinson, 1922). If record creators were to self-consciously create records for posterity, in Jenkinson's view, the possibility of historical objectivity and representation of truth would be placed in jeopardy. The evidentiary nature of records is based upon historical inattention on the part of records creators and is to be interpreted by historians and scholars exclusively.

Much like archives, Jenkinson's role for the archivist is also specifically defined. This definition is based on the concept of a curator who is charged with the supervision of the accumulation of records in an archive. Jenkinson's archivist spends his or her time arranging and describing records and processing new records into the collection as they arrive. The contents of the archive are decided *a priori*, as appraisal is not an archival activity in this definition. For Jenkinson, history can be written because archives create an unfiltered and unquestionable truth direct from record creators. The archivist's duties were defined primarily to safeguard the archives and maintain official custody. Secondarily, the archivist is to provide for the needs of users, who were predominately historians and other researchers (Jenkinson, 1922). The narrowly defined tasks for the archivist are focused on the archival material as a whole, not on policies, specific uses, or facilities.

Jenkinson prescribes a passive role for the archivist. According to Jenkinson (1922), "Merely to save archives so important for local history by offering them an asylum is a work of piety and usefulness" (p. 40). Jenkinson notes that an archivist should be interested in archives for their own sake, not to change the course of history. For Jenkinson, the maintenance of archives is self-evident. Archivists should not interfere with records because the records were created without the archivist's involvement. For Jenkinson, this is the only way to ensure objective evidence in the archive.

In Jenkinson's paradigm, this definition of limited influence is key to the maintenance of objective, therefore authentic, records: "[The archivist's] work consequently is that of physical and moral conservation and his interest is an interest in his Archives, not as documents valuable for providing this or that thesis" (Jenkinson, 1922, p. 125). Tschan sums up Jenkinson's definition of the archivist's role as one of essentially an advisor to records creators who at most attempts to establish record keeping rules. The sum of these activities is Jenkinson's role of the archivist. This classic role, in which the archivist is a keeper of records, not an interpreter or official arbiter of historical importance, can be viewed as the basis for objective information in the archive. If Jenkinson's goal was to present the most objective truth to archival users, the best way to maintain the sanctity of the evidence in records would be to ensure that archivists were not able to modify the records in the course of their work. Jenkinson's archivist seeks to know the collection without becoming invested in the collection itself.

The truth in Jenkinson's archive is purely objective. The circumstances of action are preserved through the relationship between records as expressed by virtue of each record included in the archive in its own place. For archivists to interpret the intention or meaning of a record would be to change the course of the possibility of writing history. Throughout his Manual, Jenkinson refers to his goal of the creation archives that continue the intellectual and informational characteristics of archives of the past. He remarks that the archives of the past have served users and archivists well and that the changes in contemporary records, including technology and bulk, should not affect archival principles. Jenkinson assumes that the same work will be asked of archivists in the future as was asked in the early 1920s.

Jenkinson's discussion of the proper role for the archivist may seem, at the beginning of the 21st century, very limited. In fact, these limits themselves were, at the time, highly innovative in their own right. By creating limits for the role of the archivist in keeping archives, Jenkinson takes some of the first explicit steps in defining the archival profession. Muller, Feith, and Fruin were professional archivists but wrote their manual for people who spent some of their time working in an archive. Jenkinson, on the other hand, worked within the context of growing national and local records offices that were increasingly staffed by trained professionals. Often, these professionals worked in relative isolation, but were required to carry out the standardized work of government mandate. Jenkinson was required to explicitly state the limits for archivists in dealing with records in their institutions. These first steps were cautious, but nonetheless, Jenkinson explicitly defined the professional expectations for archivists in his Manual. These expectations include a commitment to the archive, the ability to work with archival records, to describe, and arrange them without modifying them, and to keep official custody of them as closely as possible. These statements constituted the first in the process of professionalization for archivists as a group.

Jenkinson acknowledges the fact that archives and the agencies that create them do not remain static and discusses five ways in which archives can change without affecting the integrity of the records. The first is that archives can die out. There is little that can be done in this situation except to steer records toward the second possibility, which is for the records to be reabsorbed into the class from which the archive originated. The third possibility for change in the archive is for the functions of the archive to pass from it to another entity, most ideally, another archive. The fourth possible change is for the functions of the archive to take place under a new name. This would be the case for entities that undergo reorganization and would most likely involve the closing of one record group and the beginning of another with the new name. The final possibility for change is if the original connection a set of records had to the entities in which they were created was ever lost. This is perhaps the most difficult change in the list as it is somewhat subjective as to the integrity of the connection between archive and originating entity, but the possibility remains.

In all of Jenkinson's possibilities for change in the archive, the most important aspect of each change is the custody of the records. Indeed, custody is one of the defining characteristics of Jenkinson's archival theory. It is both the fact and the nature of custody upon which Jenkinson relies to define the authenticity and impartiality of the archive. In this case, custody is defined differently than the legal definition of the time (Jenkinson, 1922). Jenkinson stresses the evidentiary nature of archives in his theory, so it is logical that other definitions would also be juridically based.

In Jenkinson's definition, unbroken and controlled official custody ensures the authenticity of the information in archived records. Continuous custody is also a defense against forgery and other maladies that would be detrimental for archives' legal uses. For Jenkinson, the ideal is an *"unblemished line of responsible custodians"* (italics in original) (Jenkinson, 1922, p. 10-11). In order to maintain an unbroken line of custody, the contents of the archive should never leave official channels of communication or storage.

But Jenkinson has not placed these theoretical limits upon the archivist for arbitrary reasons. Jenkinson's archival theory holds impartiality and authenticity of records as two basic characteristics of archival material. These two concepts are the root of Jenkinson's argument against subjectivity in archival work. For Jenkinson, impartiality is rooted in the notion that archival records are created for a different reason than they are used later. Because records should be used for different purposes than that for which they were created, they cannot give false information. Jenkinson explains: "Provided, then, that the student understand their administrative significance, [records] cannot tell him anything but the truth" (Jenkinson, 1922, p. 12). The guarantee that the records in the archive contain true information is based upon the notion that there has been no alteration or selection of a point of view by anyone involved with the records. Jenkinson bases his distaste for subjective appraisal on the notion that it creates false archives that are collections created by individuals, not natural accumulations of records created by entities.

Though Jenkinson worked with medieval and contemporary records, his theoretical orientation is empirical and dedicated to modern concepts of truth. His commitment to truth and progress is steadfast: "Archives, if conserved with fidelity and used with intelligence, give us the best chance of arriving at the facts, at undiluted Truth. And it is for the maintenance of truth as the only sure basis of Conduct that we are now fighting" (Jenkinson, 1922, p 195). Jenkinson's orientation toward progress and correctness is in line with British historians' empiricism and devotion to the writing of scientific history in the early 20th century. His Manual is written from an innovative point of view, especially in its approach and topic. It shared its theoretical orientation with the group of historians who contributed to the British Economic and Social History of the World War Series, a series of historical works completed soon after the end of the war concerned with what was then contemporary history of World War I. This series of publications was written from a perspective that "involved a new attitude towards those two ideals which historians have sought to emphasize, consistency and objectivity" (Bulkley, 1922, p. ix). The "scientification" of archival theory and practice was understood to be a bridge from the heavily humanities-based backgrounds of most archivists to an empirical orientation. These changes took place during a watershed time in the study of history in which objectivity in historical writing became somewhat controversial. Eventually, Becker and Beard's relativism would fall out of favor, with subjectivity partially viewed to be at fault for the rise of fascism in Europe leading up to World War II.

As the Manual turns to appraisal theory and destruction of archives and the practical execution of that theory, Jenkinson does not allow any subjective decisions to be made. This is probably due to his focus and experience with medieval records, which would have familiarized Jenkinson with situations in which he must deal with varied qualities of previous archival decisions to create a contemporary whole. It is clear why permanently removing records from the archive were never part of his theory. If one were presented with an archive of "selected records," neither the archivist nor the archival user would really truly know what records were in the archive in the past.

Selective Reinforcement and Increased Control

A discussion of subjectivity in Jenkinson's theories is one of negative space. Jenkinson sought to eradicate the subjective in archival decision-making. While the general outline of Jenkinson's arrangement theory was based in the Dutch work, there were a few differences as well. Specifically, Jenkinson did not recommend the reorganization of older archival material to match contemporary trends in arrangement. Once records have been assigned a position in the archive, that place cannot be changed without affecting the context of all the records that surround it in a *fonds*. Jenkinson took further issue with the backbone/skeleton model found in the Dutch Manual. This model propounds that there is one master series of resolutions to which all others are attached (Jenkinson, 1922). The disagreement between paradigms illustrates the development, though subtle and contrary to much of Jenkinson's work, of subjectivity in the theory of archives. Where the Dutch Manual prescribed a basic procedural model for all archives in a nation, Jenkinson, less than 25 years later, argued that the enforcement of a set such guidelines is counterproductive and that *fonds* should be defined on their own terms (Jenkinson, 1922, p. 87). With such definitions, it becomes easier to see how Jenkinson would not approve of subjective appraisal decisions for records that had already passed into the archive and retained by the records creator and archivist.

With such stringent definitions and requirements for records, archives, and the careers of archivists, Jenkinson's overall archival theory is logical, internally consistent, and unforgiving. Appraisal is perhaps the most famous victim of Jenkinson's theory. The popular concept is that Jenkinson promotes keeping everything, which is the only way to ensure the authenticity and impartiality of the archive. What is examined less frequently is the way Jenkinson denies appraisal. Understanding how this important archival concept is denied is an important part of a discourse on the development of appraisal theory as many contemporary objections to similar changes have roots in Jenkinson's theory.

Jenkinson is categorically opposed to the concept altogether since appraisal and its practical cousin, destruction, interrupt the context and interrelated nature of archival records. His goal for archives is based upon the notion that archives should contain the same type of information in the same manner as archives of the past and remain of a manageable size in terms of the amount of records (Jenkinson, 1922). Jenkinson's goal is for the professional archivist to be a keeper of records, not an interpreter of history. He blames attempts by archivists to make material available for use too quickly as motivation, in part, for subjective appraisal decisions. The result is material separated from its original context and which has lost some of its meaning. In addition, Jenkinson warns against keeping individual documents, whether in official or private custody, as singular museum pieces. This practice denies not only the individual record its context, but changes the authenticity of the other records in the *fonds* in which the special record was originally created.

While much of Jenkinson's archival theory presented in the Manual may seem rigid and prescriptive, Jenkinson notes that the concepts contained in the work are ideals and that compromise is inevitable. Jenkinson advocates for broad methodological guidance in the form of theory because each archival collection is unique and its problems are specific. Jenkinson (1922) is convinced that a general adherence to objective goals will prove successful: "In most sciences and arts it will be found that special cases can be satisfactorily met by any one who combines a sound theory with ordinary common sense and both with practical experience" (pp. 18-19). He also acknowledges the impending increase in subjectivity in archival practice, especially in arrangement activities, but does not promote the rearrangement of old archival material. Jenkinson's limitation on subjectivity, while more liberal than past theories, are nonetheless well-defined. The acknowledgment of increased subjectivity in archival theory extends to the archivist's consideration of the archive as a whole: "He himself must be the judge of what is required and should allow no external interference..." (Jenkinson, 1922, p. 107). In this case, external interference would include possible future research interests for the archive or the use of the archive by historians. However, this example illustrates Jenkinson's willingness to allow archivists to begin to make decisions based on what is best for the archive. While Jenkinson would most likely argue that decisions made with logical reasoning are, indeed, best for the archive, this is a different approach to subjective decision making than that of Muller, Feith, and Fruin in the Dutch Manual.

Jenkinson's Critics

Many of Jenkinson's critics are able to view his theories from the privileged position afforded by hindsight. Criticisms of Jenkinson's theories emerged only after other paradigms had been created and established as viable. These critics were enabled to do their work because of Jenkinson's emphasis on the professionalization of archival work. Though the role of the archivist Jenkinson prescribes is limited, his concepts are responsible for the expansion and redefinition of the archival profession. Jenkinson's work also created a solid basis for the creation of modern records, strong appraisal theory, and the concepts of records management that would dominate archival work in the United States during the Cold War.

The limits of the role of the archivist in Jenkinson's theory were difficult for an international audience to maintain. As the 1920s would become a celebratory decade of excess, the time between the two World Wars being economically and culturally prosperous for many until the Great Depression in 1929, archivists and the population in general were not held in check by notions of propriety. As culture changed and accelerated—for instance—as individual freedom and cultural relativism increased, subjectivity became less of a distasteful concept and more of accepted epistemological point of view. An example of this is the work of historians Charles Beard and Carl Becker. Both men worked to illustrate that history was a matter of interpretation by an individual. Judgment of action was viewed as relative to the actor, not necessarily as inherently good or evil in the universe.

Technologically, the landscape was also in a state of constant change. Where, in the past, fewer records were created due to technological and personnel limitations, Jenkinson's theories were quickly tested by unprecedented amounts of records created on a local and national level. Technological change became a direct challenge to Jenkinson's theories, forcing archivists to look for new answers to problems of record bulk and challenges posed by changing demands on the archive by both citizens and governments. Theorists also began to write about the impact of technological change leading up to World War II. An example of this reconsideration of the impact of technology on culture is Walter Benjamin's 1936 essay, *The Work of Art in the Age of Mechanical Reproduction* which sought to understand recontextualized meaning of art in light of industrial change.

Considering the rapid change in communication technology and the many innovations in the mechanical reproduction of records, reevaluation of the archivist's work might be appropriate. Jenkinson (1922) is somewhat aware of this, as he notes that looking to the past continues the problems of the past as well (p. xi). Regardless, Jenkinson defines the information found in archives as the same, whether ancient or contemporary. He asks "is there anything in the modern fashion of making Archives which should exclude them from the operation of general rules as to archive treatment?" (Jenkinson 1922, p. 91). Though Jenkinson attempts to create an archival theory that will serve the records and archives first, he himself laments the work of previous archivists. He explains: "Unfortunately the earlier custodians of the Public Records in England (for example) have not always been as reasonable as we could wish in their treatment of their charges" (1922, p. 32). What prohibits archivists after Jenkinson from leveling the same criticism of his work?

The combination of all of these changes: cultural, historical, and technological, quickly shifted the demands of the archive. As new historians completed their studies under the tutelage of professors who taught subjective methodologies in the tradition of Becker and Beard, young professionals used different types of technology with regularity, and citizens began to have different expectations and encounters with their governments, Jenkinson's ideas and ideals were reconsidered not long after they were published.

Jenkinson's role for the archivist was one set within very strict limits. The irony in his strict definition is that while Jenkinson defined what a professional archivist was, those same professionals quickly sought further expanded duties than Jenkinson's curatorial role would allow. In this regard, Jenkinson can be considered the true father of the contemporary archival profession. Subsequent archival paradigms would look to Jenkinson's concepts of the archivist's role and create new definitions that were directly in opposition to his parameters.

Jenkinson was also criticized, most vocally, by Theodore Schellenberg, for his disapproval of appraisal. As discussed below, archivists around the world, but especially in the United States, found Jenkinson's theories incompatible with the use and bulk of records they faced. Many of these records would not have even qualified as archives within Jenkinson's definition. Schellenberg and others would go on to criticize Jenkinson's narrow definitions of archives, records, and how archivists were allowed to work within these limits.

One of the criticisms of Jenkinson's theories is that they were created too late, and, as a result, existed outside of their time. According to MacNeil (1997), the focus of Jenkinson's work is on records of the past arranged and described using criteria based on a morality that can change over time. Jenkinson's Manual was responsible for reinforcing archival concepts from the Dutch Manual. It also sewed the beginnings of the definition of the archival profession. His manual would, within a few years, become a definition of an unrecognizable profession. Jenkinson's theories, which stood still in time, were published at a point when the world was only beginning to move more quickly.

Jenkinson argued in support of his theories until his death in 1961 (Ellis & Walne, 2003), convinced that his was the proper path for archivists to follow. Perhaps it is this surety that makes it easy to disagree with Jenkinson. Or perhaps it is the essential tautological nature of his theory that makes disagreement so important to a discourse on appraisal theory. An example of Jenkinson's tautologies can be found in his Manual in a discussion regarding arrangement "for the Archives cannot be understood without a knowledge of the Administration which produced them, and the history and development of that Administration is often written in the Archives; so that the process is simply that known as puzzling it out" (Jenkinson, 1922, p. 81). While this process is, in itself, probably true and inconsequential, it becomes problematic when considered in the context of Jenkinson's prescriptions regarding appraisal. If the same "puzzling it out," were applied to subjective appraisal decisions, Jenkinson would have none of it.

Conclusion

Sir Hilary Jenkinson's theory of archival management is monolithic in its presentation, implementation, and logic. Epistemologically, any complete theory is difficult to create and defend. This type of theory is important for reinforcement of previous values and theories, but it can also create a dialectic in which there are more questions than answers.

Jenkinson himself relies on logic and causality to define his archival theory, so a critical reading of his Manual should take this immanent critique as a point of departure.

While Jenkinson seeks to expand and reinforce an all-encompassing archival theory, he acknowledges that war archives are singular in their content, if not their creation. With this acknowledgment comes a willingness to treat war archives a bit differently than other archives. This is an instance in which the archivist may put more subjective decisions forward and the results would undergo a different type of scrutiny due to the circumstances of impermanence and timeliness. These unspecified exceptions do beg the question of the effectiveness of objectivity in archival theory, however. If archives are valuable because their content and context are singular, then it is nearly impossible for every archive to not be a special case.

The goal of reading archival theory critically is to understand how appraisal theory developed over time, to poke and prod at the gaps in thinking, to see where new ideas can come from in the future and to understand how familiar ideas developed in the past. Jenkinson addresses the evaluation of the past in a positive manner: "In a word we can criticize the Past only if it failed to keep up to its own standard of values" (Jenkinson, 1922, p. 119). While this critical reading of Jenkinson's theory is not intended to evaluate, it is intended to investigate. Jenkinson's distaste for appraisal is, using his criteria of consistency within a discourse, theoretically very sound. The discourse then becomes one of a greater context in which one asks when the effects of history have been felt long enough to warrant reevaluation and change.

While Jenkinson strives for correctness in his archival theory, he neglects to take into account the randomness of history itself. As Tschan (2002) discusses in a footnote, "The great irony is that the very records which prompted Jenkinson to examine the problems of bulk and archival appraisal had their ultimate disposition settled by German bombs: 60 percent of the records of the first World War were destroyed [during World War II]" (p. 177). There is no amount of appraisal, subjective or otherwise, that can save archives from destruction if the records themselves are targets during conflict, military or civil.

Criticism aside, Jenkinson's contributions to archival theory have been enormous. Through reinforcement of concepts first published in the Dutch Manual, Jenkinson's Manual created a theoretical guide for archivists in the early-to-mid 20th century to follow in their work. The reinforcement of the importance of original order helped Jenkinson create war archives that reflected the way in which the government created and used records that gave historians more context with which they could complete their work.

Jenkinson's denial of appraisal and subjectivity in the archive is famous. His justifiably stubborn stance on appraisal's theoretical validity continues to affect archival work today. Jenkinson's dedication to objectivity in both theory and practice is admirable.

Most importantly, Jenkinson's Manual explicitly began the discussion of the role of the archivist and its professional status as a discipline distinct from the study and writing of history. Poised on the edge of drastic changes in culture, government, and technology, Jenkinson's definition became the basis for contemporary archivists and their professional discourse.

5. Modern Records: T. R. Schellenberg and *Modern Archives*

Introduction

Theodore Roosevelt Schellenberg, an archivist who worked most of his career in the federal archives of the United States, published *Modern Archives: Principles and Techniques* in 1957 and changed the archival profession in new and unforeseen ways. Viewed in the profession as a pragmatist, concerned with the efficiency of archival operations, Schellenberg wrote his archival theory from a different perspective than previous European theorists. The main focus of Schellenberg's theoretical work was written from a records management perspective rather than from the perspective of a keeper of records. Schellenberg's work in archival theory and the archival profession had a great impact among archivists, especially those professionals in the United States. His own title, *Modern Archives*, is the definitive name for this period in archival theory in that it epitomizes the modernization of archival practice and culture during the early postwar period in the United States.

The author himself viewed *Modern Archives* to be a step in the movement toward an archival profession in the United States (Jones, 2002). Records in the United States were understood to involve different issues than European records. Schellenberg sought to create a theoretical approach that would accommodate the perceived differences rather than adapt European practices for use in the United States. His most famous disagreement regarding theory was between himself and Sir Hilary Jenkinson. At almost every turn, one can contrast the two theories. The differences are most pronounced when one examines the discrepancies between the two in terms of appraisal and custody.

Along with the difficulties of avoiding adapting past, foreign practices to archives in the United States, Schellenberg faced unprecedented amounts of unsorted documents during the time in which his theories were created. In fact, Tschan (2002) remarks that bulk was indeed the defining characteristic of modern records of the time. Faced with an ever-increasing number of records created by the federal government and its agencies, Schellenberg really had no choice other than to embrace appraisal theories and methodologies that resulted in decreased numbers of records retained in archives. In fact, he became a pioneer of appraisal theory, heralded as the father of archival appraisal (Cook, 1999). Schellenberg's unique position necessitated that his approach to appraisal theory be one developed in terms of a large federal government. This is in contrast to democratic and monarchical European governments, which were required to keep archives containing feudal and even older church-based records. The result is a theory Schellenberg pioneered based on a record's lifecycle in combination with the concepts of records management. Most importantly, Schellenberg required a theory that held efficiency as a primary goal.

Schellenberg's theories were well received in post-war era United States, so much so that Bantin (1998) notes that Schellenberg's appraisal theory was the most successful and widely adopted archival theory in the United States. Schellenberg's theories were successful in the wake of not only an increased number of records, but also within the context of broadened social perspectives that expanded the definition of archival value based upon interest and research value. Various groups, including veterans, women, and people of color were beginning to gain more and different power in the United States during the post-war era. Schellenberg's theories were created in this shifting social landscape, in part in reaction to the demands of social historians and sociologists who presented new and challenging research interests to the government's archives. Schellenberg remained modest about his challenges to European archival theory, especially in terms of appraisal. He noted: "I do not believe that American methods of handling modern public records are necessarily better than those of other countries; they are merely different" (Schellenberg, 1956/2003, p. xviii).

Modernizing the Contemporary

As was the case with the development of the previous two theoretical paradigm shifts in archival theory, Schellenberg's theories were published during a time of social, cultural, and historical change. During the New Deal, World War II, and the post-war era in the United States, the creation of records increased exponentially (Jones, 2002). The growth of the government and the ever-expanding role it played in the lives of its citizens during this time resulted in large, unimagined increases in the number of records created, used, and saved. The best example of the type of government growth that affected archives is the New Deal.

The New Deal, a set of extremely important and highly influential relief programs for the United States set in place by President Franklin D. Roosevelt between 1933 and 1937, was nearly solely responsible for the new role the federal government played in the lives of its citizens during the middle of the 20th century. With programs such as the Works Progress Administration, Farm Security Administration, Civilian Conservation Corps, and Tennessee Valley Authority, the federal government created what is now known as a broker state by inserting itself between businesses and consumers ("New Deal," 2007). Along with regulating the market to favor the fair application of competition, the New Deal also provided new social services through the Social Security Act and National Labor Relations Act, among others. These programs ensured citizens' rights were protected in old age and infirmity, and at work, respectively. The effect of an unprecedented expansion of government at all levels was not only an extremely large increase in the number of records, but also new and different uses of records by a motivated set of citizens. While the New Deal increased the government's need and capacity to create records, the total war of World War II created new ways of dealing with records. Mechanical reproduction, widespread use of the typewriter, and a decentralized system of record keeping combined to create massive amounts of documentation of the government's activities.

The industrialization of urban centers in the United States as war manufacturing increased required that production levels be maintained after the conclusion of the war to avoid a continuation of the Great Depression. The G.I. Bill of Rights, signed into law in 1944, created a more democratized higher education system and home ownership opportunities for veterans who returned from fighting. The baby boom began with increased population and prosperity for many in the United States. All of these shifts meant change for many aspects of life in America. As more people were able to participate in urban and suburban living, buy and consume durable and temporary goods, the American Dream was on its way to becoming a possible reality for many (Chafe & Sitkoff, 1991).

The post-war years were also a time of increased value placed on science, especially in regard to the exploration of space. With the Cold War well underway, the development of space travel fueled scientific education and military-sponsored development of new technologies. Government funding for scientific endeavors reached unprecedented proportions, especially after the Soviet launch of Sputnik in 1957 (Chafe & Sitkoff, 1991).

The faith in science as salvation for the United States developed a unity of cultural thought, especially in terms of war in Europe and the development and use of nuclear energy for weapons. After the relativism of the inter-war years, unity and certitude became the dominant force in American culture. The 1950s became the era of *The Man in the Gray Flannel Suit*, families moved to the suburbs and began to consume at unprecedented rates to keep up with manufactured need and their neighbors' purchasing patterns. Scientific thought—logical, empirical, and unified—influenced the writing of history along with many other aspects of intellectual life at the time. Scientific history and progress became the goal and motivation for many academics after the disagreements over relativism and isolationism around the globe. The unity of thought defined value in a systematic manner. Unquestionable certitude in progress and a conception of linear historical movement created further desire for cause and effect in historical discourse. One could not but have faith in the future because the immediate past had been so horrific.

Examples of the new historical writing can be found in works such as Arthur Schlesinger Jr.'s (1949) *The Vital Center* and Daniel J. Boorstin's (1953) *The Genius of American Politics*. In a sense, both of these works attempted to repudiate the relativism of the 1920s and 1930s while creating a new, modern consensus of moral history to fight against communism and for a free market and liberal democracy. This consolidation and moralism in historical writing created changes in the demands for and uses of archival records. The new historical writing was focused on agreement and creating solidarity among historians. The result was, in part, Boorstin's American exceptionalism and a dearth of challenges to the newly minted status quo. The unfavorable view of communists during the Cold War, as typified by Senator Joseph McCarthy and the House Un-American Activities Committee, contributed to the growing interest in writing agreeable histories that reinforced a pro-American and democratic point of view.

Another product of the New Deal and the emphasis on revamped government record keeping was the establishment, in 1934, of the National Archives as an independent agency. Previous to the establishment of the new federal agency, individual government entities were responsible for keeping their own records. The consolidation of archival holdings into one agency was a bureaucratic revolution for the United States. Standardization in record keeping could be enacted with fewer possibilities for non-compliance and localization. With the newly formed National Archives, records that were created in outside of Washington, DC could be housed in the National Archives but in regional record centers. The many record centers constituted and complimented the National Archives in the capital.

During this time, archivists, the traditional keepers of the past, were bolstered by their roles and found new faith within the need to keep the past alive. H. L. White (1956/2003) discussed the value of archives at this time: "In a very real sense the governmental and public attitude towards the preservation of archives is a measure of our faith in the future" (p. xv). Why would it remain important to meticulously save its records unless society was willing to come to terms with its past? Schellenberg noted that archivists of this time owed historians a debt for their continual faith and reliance on archives to complete their research work. Archivists, according to Schellenberg, were repaying that debt through guidance in regard to collections and the publication of historical documentary sources. These actions help historians to access new, uncovered sources for historical research and writing. For Schellenberg, this was an honorable, if duty-bound position for the archival profession. He characterized the archivist's role as "a hewer of wood and a drawer of water for the scholars" (Schellenberg, 1956/2003, p. 236).

While unity and repayment may have been the order of the day, the publication of Schellenberg's *Modern Archives* came during a contentious period in the early history of the National Archives in the United States. At issue was the tension that surrounded appraisal activities in the archive. Philip Bauer led one group, which was in favor of appraisal and in which Schellenberg found himself. Bauer was the Chief of Labor Department Archives at the National Archives. Bauer based his appraisal theory on four basic tenets: (a) official reference performed by government agencies, (b) protection of citizens' private rights, (c) serious research by scholars, and (d) satisfaction of genealogical and antiquarian curiosity (Shepherd, 1997). Bauer was opposed by Herman Kahn, Chief of the Division of Interior Department Archives, who did not value efficiency over objective decision making and argued that appraisal compromised records' context. Schellenberg would interpret and discuss the issues presented by both sides in *Modern Archives*.

History of an Appraiser

Schellenberg worked nearly his entire career in archives administration in the employment of the federal government of the United States. An archivist concerned with the largest problem, bulk of records, in a government that created more records than any other government before it, Schellenberg spent much of his career appraising records and creating criteria by which others could do the same. Before the publication of *Modern Archives*, Schellenberg had worked with the archives of the United States government for over 20 years (Jones, 2002).

Born in Harvey County, Kansas, in 1903, Schellenberg would devote his entire career to archives. Like many archivists of his time, Schellenberg studied to be a historian. He studied at the University of Kansas from 1924 to 1930 where he earned a Bachelor's degree and Master's degree in history. He received a doctorate in history from the University of Pennsylvania in 1934 with a dissertation about the European origins of the Monroe Doctrine.

Professionally, he worked with federal government records from 1935-1963. He held positions in the War Production Board and as Records Officer in the Office of Price Administration from 1945-1948. During his tenure in War Production Board, Schellenberg selected records for preservation from that temporary agency. In fact, one could easily make a vaild comparison between the goals of Jenkinson's war archives and Schellenberg's professional experience: both were concerned with what they respectively viewed as anomalous records situations. Another of Schellenberg's positions with the National Archives included Deputy Examiner, when he worked appraising federal records. Schellenberg was also Chief of the Division of Agriculture Department of Archives, during which time he formulate procedures for the disposal of records. Schellenberg translated his work experience into a manual on the disposition of federal records. In 1956, he would become the Director of Archival Management at the National Archives and named Assistant Archivist of the United States in 1957, a title he would hold until 1963 (Contemporary Authors Online, 2006).

In addition to his work at the National Archives, Schellenberg was very active in professional organizations. He held various positions in the Society of American Archivists, beginning in 1936. Schellenberg was also an active member of the American Historical Association during the same time period. Schellenberg had an interest in sharing his professional experiences through teaching. In 1954, he became a Fulbright lecturer in Australia and New Zealand. The result of this year abroad is the compiled text of *Modern Archives*, which originated with speeches and papers given during this time. He continued to teach at various schools that included the universities of Texas, Washington, and Columbia between 1959 and 1966.

Schellenberg became an elder statesman of the archival community. Having spent his entire archive career working for the United States government, it becomes easy to understand how efficiency could become a prime goal for any archival theory created in such an environment. The development of appraisal as an indispensable part of archival work began with Schellenberg and his professional need to reduce the number of records that waited to become part of the archive.

Efficiency in Appraisal

The text of *Modern Archives*, like the other works discussed here, is a general theoretical treatise on many aspects of archival work. The various facets in the current work include appraisal, arrangement, description, and preservation. While Schellenberg is often cited as the father of appraisal theory (Cook, 1999), the general tone and approach of *Modern Archives* is often overlooked. Schellenberg wrote *Modern Archives* to be used as the textbook for the summer Institutes taught at the National Archives (Jones, 2002) and therefore the work is explanatory and pedagogic.

In *Modern Archives*, Schellenberg's focus is the administration of public records and archives. His perspective is highly influenced by his professional experience and need to find new methods of working with an unprecedented bulk of records. A distinguishing characteristic of Schellenberg's theory is that his focus is clearly on contemporary records and the problems created when new records are forced to fit into old categories and processes. This is one source of the break and subsequent friction between Schellenberg and Jenkinson. While Jenkinson approached his contemporary archives from the perspective of the past, establishing principles for the future based upon tested methodology and theory from previous archives, Schellenberg moves in the opposite direction, from the future disposition of the record to his contemporary situation.

The distinguishing characteristic of Schellenberg's approach is that his appraisal and evaluation criteria are created from a records management approach to archiving. In *Modern Archives,* he explains, "Record management is thus concerned with the whole life span of most records" (Schellenberg, 1956/2003, pp. 33-4). Though Schellenberg's appraisal innovations may have come from a records keeping perspective, his overall theories are well-grounded in traditional archival principles that include the organic nature of archives, the implementation of *respect des fonds* as a concept in terms of arrangement, the understanding that archives were created in the course of activities to accomplish specific purposes, and that archives be kept safe from damage (Tschan, 2002; H. L.White, 1956/2003).

Schellenberg's theoretical innovations, such as a record keeping perspective and reliance on appraisal, were understood to be an attempt to connect the archival profession to allied groups of professionals like historians and librarians. Though a portion of *Modern Archives* is dedicated to the precise delineation of the differences between librarians and archivists, this is done as a means to separate the professions into distinct disciplines but maintain their vital relationship. Cook (1999) notes that Schellenberg was also motivated to consider researchers' needs and expand the types, if not necessarily the number, of records in archives and available for research. The effect of this expansion was to lower the influence of institutional bias in the archive that had been instilled by the admission of narrowly defined record types under previous paradigms.

Through his implementation of record keeping strategies, especially in terms of appraisal, Schellenberg focused much of his work on contemporary records. Since the bulk of records created by the federal government of the United States increased by a magnitude of 10 between the Civil War and World War I, tripled again between World War I and the Depression, and then during World War II alone, created two-thirds of the previous total amount of records each year, a focus on control of new records in the archive was worthwhile and necessary (Schellenberg, 1956/2003). This focus is the defining split between the traditional archival theory of previous paradigms and Schellenberg's appraisal theory. This innovation is predicated on the custodial model for past records while implementation of Schellenberg's theories create distinct archives that consist nearly exclusively of modern records.

There are also similarities between Schellenberg's innovative appraisal theory and past practice. Schellenberg himself equates the study of record keeping methods for the creation of modern archives with the study of diplomatics for the creation of medieval archives (1956/2003). Both modes of inquiry relate to the entities and individuals who created records so that the records' context can be preserved for future research. They both also seek to understand how archives can represent information as closely as possible to how it was kept and used when that information was in active use.

While Schellenberg's reputation has been characterized as practical and pragmatic, *Modern Archives* offers what the author understands to be a first step toward the creation of a new archival profession in the United States based on innovative principles (Schellenberg, 1956/2003). The federal government in the United States created the National Archives nearly 160 years after independence from England. It is therefore understandable that a professional archivist in the 1950s would characterize the archival profession in the United States as in its early development. Perhaps due to the relatively young archival program in the United States, Schellenberg notes a distinct lack of a singular, coherent archival theory to guide archivists through their work. Instead of defining the archive (place) and archives (collections of documents) as two separate concepts, Schellenberg advocates for a conflation of the two in the United States. It is this type of expanded possibility for experimentation, especially in appraisal theory, that established a modern archival discourse. This is in contrast to previous paradigms in which their authors focused on the publication of edicts from archival theorists to practicing archivists.

The definition of the archive in the United States has been influenced, from the official beginning of the National Archives, by government requirements and the information needs of citizens. Schellenberg's definitions of archives were conceived within the context of the need to make records available for citizens' democratic participation in government. The evidentiary and cultural uses of records, as defined more in-depth below, were utilized in new and unprecedented ways, in part due to Schellenberg's innovations. The dedication to keeping archives was a determinant for the success of a country as a whole. The eminent historian C.M. Andrews noted that archives in the United States are required for its citizens to master their own history and as a mark of the country's own level of civilization (Schellenberg, 1956/2003).

Andrews' support of archives in the United States denotes the understanding that archives are not just records of national achievements, but that the archive is a record of the processes used to obtain those achievements. Schellenberg took a pragmatic approach and outlined four primary reasons to keep archives. The first is to increase government efficiency. This is basically an information retrieval motivation. If records are difficult to find, they can be lost or functionally useless. Schellenberg's second motivation is cultural, specifically the accountability of the government to its citizens. The information regarding government action, required in order to maintain a balance of power, was established during the French Revolution when the revolutionaries made all records of the new government available to the public. The third motivation is personal interest, a desire to save and remember portions of what has come before and faded into the past. The fourth and final reason is that governments require records in order to operate. This is an official and pragmatic motivation to keep archives as well, one that is related to the first motivation of government efficiency.

Inherent in the four motivations for maintaining archives is the notion of appraisal. When contrasted with Jenkinson's definition of the archive that focuses on custody and complete documentation, it is easy to see the differences in the foci of archives in the United States and England. In Schellenberg's conception, appraisal is part of the definition of the archive, not a task applied to records already in the archive. Further, Schellenberg's definition of the modern archive was broad and far reaching. His definition included: acceptance of records that are often indeterminate in content; that modern archives can be variously arranged; that each archive is unique in character; that the contents of modern archives contain selected materials chosen due to their evidential or informational values, because of their significance in the documentation of a subject or activity; that the records themselves have value in either informational or evidentiary terms; and that the records are valuable for any number of purposes (Schellenberg, 1956/2003).

Specifically, the definition of the archive was predicated on the work Schellenberg did in the National Archives. His experience working with federal archives was highly influential in the recontextualization and redefinition of archives in the United States. The two essential elements in this new definition were that records are produced during official activities and that the value of records in the archive is different than the reason the records were created (Schellenberg, 1956/2003). The custody requirement, a major source of conflict between Jenkinson and Schellenberg, is absent.

Schellenberg's new definition of the modern archive becomes records that "are adjudged worthy of permanent preservation for reference or research purposes" and records that "have been selected for deposit in an archive" (Schellenberg, 1956/2003, p. 16). Coincidental to this definition, the National Archives sought to serve the following fields of knowledge in order of importance: public administration, diplomatic history, national history, economic history and theory, demography, biography and genealogy, and physical science. These fields were served by the National Archives performing the functions of: disposition activities, which included appraisal, reappraisal, destroying records of no value; preservation and arrangement activities; description and publication activities; and reference service activities. The information provided by these activities and functions focused on serving the relations between citizens and government, relations between citizens that are affected by relations with the government, and official government activity (Schellenberg, 1956/2003).

Externally, Schellenberg's definition, service areas, functions, and focus of work for modern archives were all created to help keep the government operating efficiently while being able to respond to increased demands both from citizens and from the amount of records eligible for the archive. Schellenberg reinforced the last point by including appraisal in his definition of modern archives as archivists in the United States required an archival system that would allow them to add new records to series and new series to archives on a continual basis (Schellenberg, 1956/2003). This illustrates another split with Jenkinson, in that archivists in the United States worked with active as well as inactive records, whereas Jenkinson concentrated on the creation of archives of the future that are structured like archives of the past.

New definitions of archives require new definitions for records, the pieces that make up the whole. Schellenberg's definition of an archival record is fairly succinct. It includes all material from a public institution created by the normal business or legal transactions of a government or business. This material must also be preserved as evidence or for informational value (Schellenberg, 1956/2003, p. 16). This definition is intentionally broad, but does include a provision of appropriateness, a provision that allows for increased subjectivity in archival decision-making. A further innovation Schellenberg put forward in his definition of records is that archival records can be on any media. As media of records diversified throughout the 20th century, archivists acknowledged the existence of media other than paper as containing archival information. This recognition changed archival information into archivable records.

If Schellenberg's new definition of records includes the necessity of appraisal, what is to keep groups of records together in an archive? Schellenberg answers this question by posing three specific criteria for the integrity of records: that records be kept together, in original order, and not undergo unauthorized destruction (Schellenberg, 1956/2003). This last point is the key to understanding the subtle difference between accumulation and collection, between appraisal and destruction. The authorization requirement allows the archivist increased control in the destruction of records, which should not be undertaken lightly.

Most famously, in terms of the definition of records, Schellenberg is known for his double, or split, value system. The primary value of a record, according to Schellenberg's definition, is evidentiary: does this record show evidence of action? The secondary value, nearly equally as important, is for research: would a researcher want to use this record to understand more about the context of its creation? While the acceptance of these definitions is currently debatable, it is interesting to note that Schellenberg describes primary value as more easily determined once a record is inactive but the secondary value of a record as more dependent upon its context. He further defines secondary value as more important predominantly for large groups of people. The result is that economists and sociologists become the primary users of records retained for their secondary value in this theoretical model. Both of these disciplines could, at least at the time of Schellenberg's writing, be described as attempts to implement scientific principles in the social sciences.

As the uses of archives became more scientific, Schellenberg's conception of appraisal became somewhat more subjective. Schellenberg (1956/2003) describes appraisal as determining "the value of an item in relation to other items" (p. 21). Subjectivity in making appraisal decisions is forthrightly acknowledged. Schellenberg states that the archivist's appraisal decisions "are final and irrevocable" and that the archivist should use great care when making these subjective choices: "In making value judgments, therefore, the archivist must be especially sound in his analysis of the organization and function of the body with which he deals" (Schellenberg, 1956/2003, p. 21). In contrast to previous theorists, Schellenberg allows the archivist much more power and latitude in making appraisal decisions. This is perhaps due to Schellenberg's conception of the archive as ultimately beholden to the entity that created the records: an irresponsible archivist will be held in check by the sponsoring entity. Regardless, these descriptions of appraisal activities stand in stark contrast to any conception of the archivist as a passive keeper of records. Schellenberg's definition of appraisal takes the notion of subjectivity somewhat for granted and assumes that many archival decisions will be made by an individual archivist who endeavors to make the most logical, though not necessarily objective, decision possible.

In Schellenberg's paradigm, the role of the archivist becomes incontrovertibly that of a unique professional who is expected to receive specialized training separate from both historians and librarians. In fact, *Modern Archives* originated as a textbook for Schellenberg's course at the Institute in the Preservation and Administration of Archives (Jones, 2002). The creation of the professional records manager further distinguished the professional role of the archivist and allowed for enhanced autonomy. For Schellenberg, the archivist was able to bridge the gap between record creators, represented by the records manager, and users, typically historians. Schellenberg's professional reclassification and increased autonomy for the archivist was an innovative and unique approach that helped solidify the notion of the archival professional and broke from previously defined roles.

In developing his appraisal theory, Schellenberg investigated the various theories of other countries including England, France, Germany, and the Netherlands. In *Modern Archives,* he frequently refers to theories and practices in each of these countries. If Schellenberg's theory is a departure from the accepted norm, it is undertaken intentionally and consciously. For example, Schellenberg discusses, in-depth, the registry systems of these European countries in an attempt to illustrate how subjective appraisal is not appropriate for each system. In this case, he singles out England's registry system as particularly incompatible.

The key to understanding Schellenberg's appraisal theory is twofold. The first is the concept of the record manager. This position in an entity is a type of intermediary between the entity and the archivist who enacts the records retention schedules and disposal of records that do not have archival value. While the records manager works with the archivist to implement appraisal decisions, the records manager does not make appraisal decisions on his or her own. The benefit of this position in regards to appraisal is that a records manager works closely with the records creators and can concentrate on the detailed work of records management while the archivist is free to focus on the accurate depiction of the entity's context on a broad scale. The records manager is also vital to the operation of a decentralized archival system like the one employed by the federal government in the United States in which each department maintains its own archive. In this case, decentralization makes a central registry unnecessary.

The second important concept in Schellenberg's appraisal theory is decentralization itself. With each department in the federal government keeping its own records, the National Archives are free to collect records that are concerned with federal issues as a whole. This decentralized system may seem unwieldy but indeed is held in check by the availability of mechanical duplication (Schellenberg, 1956/2003). Because archivists have the ability to make copies of documents for informational purposes, the precise location of the original becomes less important. This is the case unless the document or series has historical value. In the case of a decentralized structure, historically important documents can be preserved more easily as they are fewer in number.

To achieve a decentralized system of record keeping, Schellenberg promotes the notion that archivists should work with groups of records in context rather than individual records in order to better reflect the activities of records creators. This concept is familiar from the Dutch Manual and Jenkinson's work. While the information archive users may want is specific and contained in single documents, the archivist is concerned with recreation of the whole, the context in which those records were created. The focus on groups of records also alleviates the impact of bulk on the archivist who is concerned with the appraisal of groups of records in context rather then considering each record individually.

Schellenberg expands the relationship between records creators and archivists as he encourages archivists and records managers to collaborate with records creators to determine the secondary value of records. For Schellenberg, this collaboration does not interfere with the authenticity of archives as it might for other theorists. In an effort to reduce bulk and reflect the work of records creators, Schellenberg's proposal is useful, precisely as an effort. He further advocates for these appraisal activities to be based on value to the archive user, the recipient of the secondary value of a record, not the individual record creator. This is a transformation of the value of archival records that takes the point of view of the records creator and places emphasis on the value of the record to a potential user. This shift in the definition of value is important. Schellenberg encourages archivists to make subjective decisions based on their evaluation of how records will be used in the future. A change in the designation of records is a major paradigm change in appraisal theory. In fact, it is the very same transformation that Jenkinson argued against in his defense of a passive role for the archivist.

The paradigm shift is not change for the sake of change. According to Tschan (2002), the change in the point of view in terms of the valuation of records is what transforms records into archives, according to Schellenberg's theory. The stark contrast to Jenkinson's negligible difference between archives and records is important. Schellenberg's theories are an attempt to create archives that contain useful records that have research value and are made available for use. This goal necessitates the valuing of records based on subjective notions of future research interest. According to Schellenberg, the archivist is able to judge secondary value due to familiarity with the types of information users seek within the archive. The result of the acceptance of increased levels of subjectivity in appraisal is Schellenberg's definition of the two types of value in archival records, evidential value and informational value. Evidential value is associated with representing action taken. Schellenberg(1956/2003) defines informational value as "value that depends on the importance of the matter evidenced, i.e. the organization and functioning of the agency that produced the records" (p.139).

Schellenberg's reconception of appraisal and its place in archival work redefines the role of the archivist in the creation of the archive. The new role for the archivist is an active, professional one in which the archivist works directly with records managers and records creators to select and appraise records that will become the archive. The archivist's role is further transformed in the United States as he or she is installed as a conduit between the government and its citizens. While the government in the United States has been based upon the democratic ideal of open government, the role of the archivist as an intermediary who is able to connect citizens with government information and even select information created by the government to better serve its citizens, was a new development in archival theory when Schellenberg published *Modern Archives*.

While the official role of the archivist may have been subject to a paradigm shift, the role of the federal archive in the United States remained fairly constant. From the conception of the nation during the Continental Congress through the contemporary era, the government of the United States has been supportive of publishing its own records and making these records available, with exceptions, to the public. The publication and availability of archives became federally mandated in 1934 with the creation of the National Archives and revised in 1952 with the Federal Records Act (Schellenberg, 1956/2003). The availability of records to citizens in the United States requires the archivist to become more than a keeper of records. The archivist's role is expanded to include reference activities and public service in the archive. These activities were very different from the work of the archivist in the past. Even the definition of the role of the archivist is a point of difference between Schellenberg and Jenkinson, the former favoring a more active, guiding role and the latter concerned with the protection of records from untrained or malicious use.

Perhaps because of their more integrated interaction with users of the archive, archivists in the United States are well prepared to determine likely future research interests in their appraisal activities. In 1948, past president of SAA Philip C. Brooks noted that archivists in the United States had accumulated knowledge as to the type of records that researchers were interested in for their work (Schellenberg, 1956/2003). It is possible, of course, that this notion was due to solipsistic short-sightedness on the archivists' part, but it is more likely due to the development of a new professional role for the archivist that included reference work and work with records creators. Schellenberg outlines some of the basic concepts of value that archivists became familiar with over time. These concepts include records that relate to people value for the people to whom the records pertain and value for researchers based on their past work.

The role of the archivist is also impacted by the emphasis Schellenberg places on the definition and explication of the role of the records manager. In Schellenberg's conception, the records manager functions as an intermediary between records creators and the archivist. In a sense, the records manager's role is ideal for appraisal since the records manager works with records creators and is an agent of the same entity as records creators. While the archivist is able to focus on context and representation of action taken by an entity, the records manager can filter out records from eligibility for archival appraisal thereby reducing the bulk of records considered by the archivist. The intermediary function of the records manager reduces the need for the archivist to work directly with records creators. This allows the archivist to focus on the archive and the needs of its users rather than the needs of the records creators.

While Schellenberg envisions a different role for the archivist from those of the past, one constant is the archivist's devotion to truth. Schellenberg (1956/2003) modifies and questions this truth: "Archivists are thus the guardians of the truth, or, at least, of the evidence on the basis of which truth can be established" (p. 236). The truth is no longer self-evident in the archive. The archivist relies upon the interpretation of evidence found in the archive in order to establish truth. This raises the level of subjectivity in the creation of history and social science research exponentially. If the records creator, records manager, and archivist all have an opportunity to transform records or the archive through subjective means, the result is an archive of semi-subjective records that can be represented as the true evidence of an entity's action.

Letting Archival Freedom Ring

For Schellenberg, the basis of archival practice is closely related to geography. He notes that each country keeps its own records based on a different governmental system. While types of governments: democracies, monarchies, etc., may share common basic structures, their detailed archival practices will be different (Schellenberg, 1956/2003). He further specifically explains that Muller, Feith, and Fruin's and Jenkinson's archival theories did not perform well for the types of records created in the United States. The records Schellenberg concerns himself with are modern records, which, in his opinion, require very different types of theories and organization than older records, especially medieval records. H. L. White (1956/2003) agrees and notes that younger countries like the United States and Australia have very distinct records and archival needs that should be met through innovative approaches to their appraisal and retention.

Along with the role objectivity begins to take in Schellenberg's appraisal theory, past archival practices from Europe were also influential, though not at the forefront, of Schellenberg's theory. Schellenberg discusses the influence, especially of England and France, on the creation of his archival theories. An example is the fact, as mentioned above, that the discrepancy between Jenkinson and Schellenberg regarding the definition of the archive is, in large portion, one of custody and its importance in the creation of the definition itself. In fact, Schellenberg notes that, in order to fully understand another country's archival systems, one must undertake a serious study of the government and record keeping systems. He states "the literature of a particular country describing such principles and practices is frequently unintelligible to archivists of other countries unless the conditions under which the public records have been currently maintained are fully understood" (Schellenberg, 1956/2003, p. 27). The impact this has on subjectivity in appraisal theory is that it allows Schellenberg the ability to characterize subjective appraisal as a viable theoretical construct in the United States without denying the viability of other theories from around the world.

While Schellenberg's increasingly subjective appraisal theory may sound like an extension of the concept of American exceptionalism, it is worthwhile to note that Schellenberg recognizes the epistemological break his theories pose to other systems. He notes, "I do not believe that American methods of handling modern public records are necessarily better than those of other countries; they are merely different" (Schellenberg, 1956/2003, p. xviii). The subjectivity inherent in making appraisal decisions is also found in Schellenberg's definition of the archive: "It is obvious, therefore, that there is no final or ultimate definition of the term 'archives' that must be accepted without change and in preference to all others" (Schellenberg, 1956/2003, p. 15). The relativity in the definition creates an opening for further subjective decision making and appraisal in the future. As has been illustrated above, subjectivity in appraisal theory is modified somewhat by each country's unique archival theory. Each specific context makes a different response in terms of subjectivity appropriate. For Schellenberg, subjectivity is used as a tool to reduce bulk rather than a dangerous epistemological trap that could potentially cause chaos in the archive as it may have for Jenkinson.

Subjectivity is further acceptable in Schellenberg's theory because it allows for greater efficiency in reducing the bulk of records and enabling archivists to make important records available to potential archive users. In Schellenberg's theory, economy and efficiency have replaced Jenkinson's concepts of authenticity and objectivity. In another geographically based difference, the values of each nation and its government are also apparent in their respective archival theories. It may seem ironic that an archivist, whose concern with efficiency would become a defining methodological characteristic, would be more lenient in terms of allowing the archivist to make more subjective decisions in his or her work. Schellenberg's emphasis is on processing records for archival use and research. Subjective decision making, while still not the most theoretically desirable, is in fact, a byproduct of the desire to keep only the most useful records. The net effect is a networked one in which more archivists, who complete a high number of appraisal decisions individually, create well-appraised, and therefore more highly concentrated in terms of information, archives than would a centrally controlled, strictly objective approach.

The increased subjectivity in Schellenberg's appraisal theory is not boundless. One attempt to gain control over records, especially those of the military, was the standardization of forms. Even further standardization is required to ensure proper classification and filing of completed forms. For an archivist, these two activities are very important for efficient and proper archival functioning. Schellenberg's theory of records management functions through managers who set parameters and administrators who carry out the tasks. Each group is concerned with their portion of the work. The overall goals of the system are set by the highest level managers. Within this concept of efficiency lies a subjective core of classification: "filing systems furnish only the mechanical structure in relation to which records are to be arranged... This process, involving a large measure of subjective judgment, is the process of classification" (Schellenberg, 1956/2003, p. 91). So while classification is necessary for efficient functioning of the archive, it is subjective decision-making that makes this process possible. It is interesting to note as well that Schellenberg does not necessarily create a dichotomy between efficiency and subjectivity. In fact, subjective decisions are required to be made for efficient operations to take place.

Another attempt at control of records is the implementation of disposition plans. These plans operate as a type of manual and contract, which provides the basis of understanding between an agency and its archive as to what is to be kept and what is to be destroyed. So while archivists in Schellenberg's theory are allowed the latitude to make subjective decisions, specific instruments are created by archivists to ensure a balance between subjective decisions and a desired, standardized outcome.

One such outcome is clearly defined as useful information from records. According to Schellenberg, standards for informational value are relative to the use of the information itself. This is another situation in which Schellenberg departs from previous paradigms of rigid objectivity in calling for more subjective decision making in the appraisal of records: "Complete consistency in judging informational value is as undesirable as it is impossible of accomplishment. Diverse judgments may result in records on particular phenomena being preserved at particular places which are not deserving of general preservation" (Schellenberg, 1956/2003, p. 149). This is an unprecedented methodological and epistemological shift in archival theory in which subjectivity is embraced for the results it produces in terms of a broadening the scope of records and expressing various points of view.

It is important for archivists to have the ability to make such subjective decisions for many reasons, one of which is due to the fact that the archivist can be at the center of conflict. Schellenberg (1956/2003) notes: "[the archivist's] judgment on what should be made available and what should be withheld from public use is thus based on conflicting considerations, for his desire to foster free inquiry may conflict with the demands of public interest" (p. 226). Schellenberg suggests that one way to avoid potentially embarrassing situations in terms of interpretation of records is for the subjective decision-making to take place in situations other than reference work. If the archivist attempts to make subjective decisions about records under consideration by a user, the situation could be less than efficient or valuable for both parties.

The accommodations for subjective decisions are not all viewed in a positive manner in Schellenberg's theory. One example is of records creators changing the contents of their records as they become aware of the potential for the record to be archived later. Schellenberg notes that if records creators write with half of their attention toward archival representation, objective research will become impossible. With all of the changes Schellenberg has invoked with his appraisal theory, objective research is still the goal of reference work and, for the most part, the work of historians and other archive users. Schellenberg does not present his innovations in terms of subjectivity in appraisal theory as true innovation, as he holds objectivity as a goal for archivists in spite of criticisms to the contrary:

> The archivist's job at all times is to preserve the evidence, impartially, without taint of political or ideological bias, so that on the basis of this evidence those judgments may be pronounced upon men and events by posterity which historians through human failings are momentarily incapable of pronouncing. (Schellenberg, 1956/2003, p. 236)

In this case, subjectivity is still viewed as something that deserves to be accountable for its unpredictability rather than accepted or even embraced.

Schellenberg's Critics

With such broad changes in his approach to appraisal theory, Schellenberg conceived a new level of discourse in archival theory. After World War II, archivists around the world were thrust into new situations in which there could be little middle ground between attempting to remain a keeper of records and advocating for efficiency through appraisal. Controversy regarding the new paradigm abounded, even within the United States' government archives. The discourse between archivists who did not view appraisal as part of a viable archival paradigm and those who sought to modernize archival theory is one that continues as an undercurrent today. Schellenberg's critics question the wisdom of his dependence on the archivist to define future research interests and the archivists' ability to anticipate which records will fulfill those needs.

Schellenberg's most vocal critic was Jenkinson himself (Jenkinson 1956/2003). Jenkinson's criticisms against Schellenberg are a fundamental differential in the concept of archives and records. These discrepancies continue today with comparisons of the two theorists that attempt to persuade archivists one way or another (Tschan, 2002). In this context, Schellenberg's critics argue that the modern approach, the implementation of records management techniques, and the appraisal of records result in incomplete evidence of action taken. The ability and temptation to change the contents of the archive based on personal or institutional belief systems and goals is used as an example of the dangers of subjective appraisal decisions.

More contemporary criticism of Schellenberg's paradigm include the notion that the records management approach to archives creates archives of hierarchical power structures (Cook, 1999). These hierarchies recreate the power structures in place at the time of a record's creation, especially in the case of government archives. The reinforcement of hierarchies in this manner is criticized as continuing the under-representation of groups of people who already lack substantial amounts of official power. These contemporary theorists maintain that the focus of the archive should be on citizens' interactions with government entities, not the result of government action (Cook 1992). Schellenberg's modern archives, then, are criticized by both those who seek a more traditional role for the archivist and those who argue for a more active, even post-custodial role in which a record's disposition in the archive becomes a consideration at the time of its inception.

Conclusion

In *Modern Archives*, Schellenberg created a work that was both a product of and defined its own archival paradigm. Faced with unprecedented issues regarding records bulk, Schellenberg shifted the priorities of the National Archives to maintain a functional archive that could have easily been overwhelmed with records. While there are imperfections in every theory, Schellenberg was able to make a significant contribution to archival theory that would continue to be the dominant paradigm for at least the next 30 years.

Schellenberg also made significant contributions to the professionalization of archival work and the development of the archival profession. Schellenberg's willingness to make a significant break from previous archival paradigms stops short of questioning the theoretical basis of the professional opposition to appraisal. Instead, his theory focuses on the creation of pragmatic strategies that archivists can use with little modification in order to begin to make viable appraisal decisions. Schellenberg is ultimately committed to the archivist maintaining a keeper of truth role. He notes: "[the archivist's] contribution to the search for truth lies in making available the evidence that is in his possession" (Schellenberg, 1956/2003, p. 226). With the unity in thought evident during the post-war period in the United States, it is logical that a long-time and high-ranking staff person in the federal government would not necessarily be willing to promote a more radical agenda. Then again, Schellenberg's goals of economy and efficiency were not radically outside of an archival context. Through his promotion of appraisal as a viable archival principle, Schellenberg encouraged an active role for the archivist, especially in comparison to his predecessors in Europe.

The creation of an approach to archives based on records management strategies was a revolution in the role of the archivist as well. The archival profession was separated from the exclusively practical work of the archive and recognized as an independent profession through the records management approach to archival theory. This new orientation separated the intellectual and professional roles of the archivist from historians. The new emphasis became the archiving of current records rather than an emphasis on the preservation of older records. In this sense, Schellenberg adjusted the view of the archive from looking to records of the past toward looking Janus-like, to records of both the past and the future.

Schellenberg's openness to change was not an invitation for dramatic break in archival theory. Though subjectivity became increasingly accepted as part of appraisal theory and archival work, the agreed upon epistemological goal was still objective records. This was the case for both historians and archivists. When challenged with difficult epistemological times, Schellenberg (1956/2003) notes: "Historians may lose their balance, their objectivity, their attitude of suspended judgment, as they often have, in times of trouble" (p. 236). Ironically, this same criticism could be made of Schellenberg's theory if one were to find appraisal activities undesirable for lack of objectivity with the post-war explosion in records' volume as a "time of trouble." As will be discussed below, archivists who have challenged the necessity for an "attitude of suspended judgment" certainly have received various amounts of similar criticism in more recent times.

These contemporary archivists, while actively working toward the definition of a new archival paradigm, have read historical appraisal and archival theory with a critical eye. They have noted that Schellenberg's theoretical model, his system of valuation, is breaking down under new social pressures, changes in citizens' expectations of government, and technological change. They specifically point to his secondary research value as faulty (Cook, 1999). These archivists argue that the changing interface between citizens and government necessitates a deep and self-reflexive assessment of archival theory, especially appraisal, in order to create useful and viable archives.

6. Questioning Archives: Contemporary Records, Contemporary Discourses

The contemporary archival paradigm has been conceived as a self-conscious and historically aware approach to archival theory. The archivists who have established the most current paradigm have looked backward to previous paradigms and have been influenced by the work of past theorists from the Dutch Manual through Schellenberg. By means of a historical orientation, these archivists what are working to create and maintain the contemporary archival paradigm have sought to both understand and improve upon archival theories of the past.

In contrast to past archival paradigms, the contemporary archival paradigm is not the product of one theorist or archivist. The age of an individual luminary archivist who defines a paradigm has changed in favor of an interest in broad of diverse perspectives. The current paradigm is the result of a group of archivists and theorists who write from varied perspectives but who share a range of philosophical and critical values that stress context, interpretation, and critical reading as a framework to create archival theory. These archivists question the epistemological basis of archival theory, based upon the work of philosophers and critical thinkers. This approach assumes that the archive is itself a means of communication rooted predominantly in the disciplines of philosophy and historiography. It is an approach that self-consciously challenges many assumed aspects of past archival theory. Many archivists have contributed to the contemporary paradigm shift in archival theory. Five of the most prominent of these archivists are Brien Brothman, Terry Cook, Carolyn Heald, Eric Ketelaar, and Heather MacNeil.

There are four specific roots of the paradigm change that make the shift from modern record keeping to contemporary archiving very different from past changes. The first is the recognition and importance of context in culture. While contexts have played important roles in shaping previous archival paradigms, they become a major influence in the creation of the contemporary archival paradigm. So that while the cultural changes that took place between the 1960s and 1980s were influential in changing the content of the contemporary archival paradigm, contexts also influenced *how* the contemporary archival paradigm was created.

The second root of paradigm change is the fact that archivists working within the contemporary paradigm are conscious of their desire to change the paradigm through both practical experience and theoretical writing. A great deal of emphasis has been placed on creating a contemporary archival praxis, the confluence of theory and practice. Ribeiro (2001) notes that modern archives and techniques were beginning to be questioned in the 1980s. During this time, various questions were raised by an increasingly diverse group of intellectuals, including some who were trained archivists, which brings about the third root of paradigm change, the impact of critical theory, especially postmodern critical thought. Serious consideration of critical theory's impact on archival theory became more widely accepted in the late 1990s and continues into the 2000s. Widening diversity on university campuses and in the archival profession has been reflected in the diversity of records, types of archival institutions, and archivists themselves.

The fourth root of change in the creation of the contemporary archival paradigm is technology. While technological changes have been influential in past archival paradigm changes, none have had the same level of impact as those in the contemporary paradigm. The use of computers in both creating and maintaining records has brought almost all concepts in archival theory into question.

Technological, social, and cultural changes continued to move exponentially more quickly during the 1960s and 1970s in the United States and around the world. The Civil Rights, Women's Rights, Gay Rights, and anti-war movements of the 20th century, coupled with the entrenchment of the Cold War and possibility of total destruction through nuclear war, created a new cultural and social landscape that required significant shifts in records and record keeping. Archivists who established the contemporary archival paradigm continue to change and shape theoretical and practical answers to the new needs of archive users and their professional peers.

Questions of Contexts

If technological change impacted the volume of records during Schellenberg's career, the continuation of technological change at an increasingly faster pace, shifting critical landscapes, and an increased interest in social history accelerated previous changes and transformed these changes into new, unprecedented expectations for archivists and their archives. The changes in the social and intellectual context that surround the concept of the archive necessitated a response to further previously unforeseen challenges for archivists.

Technological change would eventually create new formats of information including electronic records. Governments and business would eventually adopt the computer as a means of communication and the basis for a majority of operations. The adoption of this technology would become so prevalent that it would eventually become more ubiquitous than even Jenkinson's much-maligned typewriter. Archivists would be forced to recognize these changes and reconcile their work with varied technologies. In fact, the impact electronic records have had on archivists is still in the process of being measured and understood. Digital records that have never existed in paper form have been a difficult issue for archives as many governments and organizations have moved toward publishing information and records for digital use only.

Changes in technology also impacted the study and writing of history. With access to powerful computer systems, historians were able to use archival information in new ways. Archives became repositories of not only anecdotal information but were also able to provide historians with huge amounts of newly pliable data that enabled broad, statistically based analyses of an infinite number of topics. As a result of technological change, historians were able to interpret and reinterpret archival resources in new ways and discover new patterns in lives of both historical prime movers and previously unstudied groups of people. These new possibilities also placed new and varied demands on the archive and archivists who were called upon to provide access to more records more quickly.

With cultural and technological change taking place at such high rates, critical understanding and analysis of the meaning of these changes became more imperative over time. Postmodern critical theory became one significant way for historians and other academics to engage with rapid cultural, social, and technological changes. These sometimes controversial critical theories celebrate ambiguity, tolerance, diversity, and multiple identities (Cook, 2001), the opposite of certainty, linear thinking, xenophobia, and contained identities. The postmodern framework was itself influenced by technology. Specifically, the globalization of media and commerce (Cook, 2001), created by increased reliance upon communications technology and an ever-increasing capability of computers, changed not only how communication operated, but what was said as well.

As the writing of history and critical theory were understood to be communication and therefore subject to transmission, interpretation, and criticism, archives were also implicated in this milieu as the basis for so much history and historiography. Postmodern cultural critics began to notice the archive and historians' dependence on archival records to recreate history and questioned the archive directly. Archivists have expressed a broad range of interests in terms of a professional response to these types of questions. A mixed response to postmodern criticism is logical since much of postmodernism's viability as an overarching philosophy is debatable.

Many postmodern questions of the archive stem from the questioning of metanarrative. Described by Jean-François Lyotard as a grand, cohesive all-encompassing story or account of history (Lyotard, 1979/1984), metanarratives are repositories of obscured meaning in postmodern theory. In terms of the study and writing of history, metanarratives represent the acceptance of a single authoritative history as the exclusive or even scientific truth. Criticism of metanarratives, as represented by *de facto* truth in the writing of history, became a focus for historians who worked to create histories of previously undocumented groups. Often, the techniques employed by postmodern historians include interpretation of archival records. Another approach to postmodern implementation of historical theory is to examine the archive itself.

Derrida (1995) makes one such attempt at expanding the archival paradigm, although in an oblique manner, in a short but effective book, *Archive Fever*. The work is a discussion of the ultimately manic need to save records as evidence of action taken for fear of losing the memory of that action, and by extension, the action itself. The book originated as a speech given at the Freud Museum in Vienna and as such, is a Freudian analysis of the need to archive. Archive fever is defined as the manic desire to save for fear of losing (Derrida, p. 94). This drive is so demanding and insatiable that Ketelaar (2001) interprets it to mean that life is defined by archiving as the creative agent of memory. Since archiving memory defines life so sharply, it also gives value to records it records as memories. The conscious saving of records is perceived as valuation beyond any other as the act of saving adds the highest level of value possible to the object.

While technology and critical theory had tremendous impacts upon the archive and have helped create the change in values that is the contemporary paradigm shift, by far the most significant impact on archival theory has been from the development of social history. The social movements of the 1960s and 1970s influenced the writing of social history. As diverse groups of people began to demand civil rights and recognition from groups that traditionally held power, historians began to write histories of smaller, underrepresented, and groups previously unrecognized by historians. Social history was the result of greater changes in society as a whole.

Historians began to participate in social changes and developed a new approach to the research and writing of history. Social history was a new way of writing history that sought to understand the past through the evolution of social trends, norms, and behaviors ("Social history," 2005). This was accomplished through the historical study of people in various social positions and classes, not just great men or political history. One well-known example of social history is Louise Tilly's and Joan Wallach Scott's (1978) *Women, Work and Family* that discussed women's economic contributions to family and society in 17th century England and France. The impact social history had on the research and writing of history beginning in the 1960s was immense. The study of history expanded to include the histories of ethnic groups, the working class, and the environment as just a few examples. In fact, social history would go on to supplant political history as the dominant mode of historical inquiry in the 1980s.

The changes in society that helped create interest in social histories included movements that recognized non-white, non-elites as participants in political and social consciousness: the anti-war movement, the feminist movement, the gay, bisexual, and trans-gendered movement, and the Civil Rights movement. The Civil Rights movement is one of the most important examples, in terms of archives, of these changes. Creating a broad reorganization of equality, both social and legal, the Civil Rights movement included new expectations of the public treatment of women, youth, peoples of color, Native Americans, and others who had been disengaged and disenfranchised by the traditional power structure, especially in the eyes of governments. As a result of these people's absence from traditional roles of power, the evidence of their actions had not previously been explicitly saved in the archive.

While historians began to broaden their academic interests beyond the histories of wars and leaders, students began to organize the anti-war movement to protest the Vietnam War. The anti-war movement was vital in increasing government accountability in a similar manner as the Civil Rights movement. As university campuses erupted in protest against the Vietnam War, new demands were placed on governments to justify and explain policies of aggression in various parts of the world as well to account for domestic issues. As college and university campuses around the world were overrun with sit-ins, teach-ins, and other broad-based civil disobedience, new groups of people were beginning to have their voices heard by mainstream politicians and others in power. Those who demanded power from the traditional leaders, including government and military leaders, wrote social history in a conscious manner. Eventually, the anti-war movement would be able to claim at least some responsibility in the United States' decision to withdraw its troops from Vietnam and the 26th Amendment to the Constitution, which lowered the voting age to 18. What makes the anti-war and Civil Rights movements such watersheds in terms of historical study, social history, and archives is that they were both popular movements based on the concept of government accountability.

Eventually, the mode of questioning that led to the development of social history and the anti-war movement would give rise to the application of postmodern critical theory to historical inquiry. The elevation of historiography from a relatively obscure area of interest to a full-fledged discipline created new and fertile territory for questioning the way history was written, and from whose perspective. The questioning that some historiographers undertook was based on the concept that histories were communications that were literary in nature as written documents. As such, these histories and the writing of histories were subject to interpretation. The interpretation of histories in a more literary context became known as the "linguistic turn." The linguistic turn is described as a development in Western philosophy when the focus of philosophy became concerned with language as constructing reality (Norris, 2005). When applied to history and historiography, the result is the interpretation of primary sources and the discussion of others' interpretations. The linguistic turn in history was established by Hayden V. White's *Metahistory* in 1975 in which he rejects the notion of causality in history and establishes the notion that the study of history is a form of communication which is susceptible to various interpretations.

The linguistic turn in history is one example of the type of effect postmodern critical theory has had on historical inquiry. The linguistic turn, and subsequently postmodern approaches to history, created an approach in which the role of the historian is to interpret signs (semiotics) and the meaning of history (Cook, 2001) as opposed to telling history as it happened. The viable interpretation of historical signs is heavily dependent upon deep contextual understanding of not only the historical time being studied, but also of the records and original sources that create specific historical narratives. Archivists are professionally concerned with context regardless of their orientation in terms of the linguistic turn, but the approach of the postmodern paradigm seeks to expand the breadth and meaning of context beyond its previous boundaries.

One example of postmodern history is Michael Lesy's (1973) *Wisconsin Death Trip*. This book examines the social and cultural changes of a small Wisconsin town in the 19th century. The book combines historical photography, text from original sources, and self-conscious contemporary interpretation of both sources. The combination of elements creates a willfully subjective look into the history of a "forgotten" group of people in the Midwest who may have undergone some sort of collective trauma due to their living conditions. One of the author's main points in the work is that it is not possible to determine what the psychological history of the town had been, so subjective historical interpretation and speculation are modes available to contemporary audiences.

Other examples of postmodern history include works by F. R. Ankersmit, Lawrence Stone, and Elizabeth Fox Genovese. The two latter writers are most well-known for their writing concerning the family and feminist history. The former is best known for writing postmodern historiography, the history of the study of history and its change over time.

Changes in archival work were also manifest during the end of the 20th century. As was the case with Schellenberg, and to some extent, Jenkinson, the contemporary archival paradigm has been forced to adapt to significant technological change. By virtue of the archive's place at the end of a record's lifecycle, archivists were once again forced to determine how to deal with change quickly and after technological change had already taken place.

The most obvious as well as deeply felt technological change archivists are still working to comprehend is the ubiquitous use of computers. Governments, government agencies, non-profit organizations, businesses, and archivists themselves have adopted the computer and electronic records as their main communication tool. Whether a government document is only available online or an archivist works with researchers via email, newly created records may never be seen in paper format.

The evolution of electronic records has moved quickly while archivists' ability to use and retain these types of records has not. Without a clear set of standards for formats, metadata, or a vested interest in supporting legacy programs and software on the part of market-driven companies, archivists have unfortunately been placed in an unenviable position in terms of saving electronic records. Preservation is an important and difficult in regards to non-paper records. The theoretical possibilities are nearly limitless.

One example of the possibilities for change in archival theory as a result of both technological change and the influence of social history is the definition of the record. In the past, records were defined in a narrow manner and, as such, were easily identifiable and comparable to one another. Assessment of relative hierarchical value is fairly easy with such specific definitions. Varied definitions of records necessitate different points of departure for the definition of the concept of the archive, which is more fluid in the contemporary paradigm than in the past. According to MacNeil (1994), "changing attitudes about citizens' rights to information have eroded their special status as public resources of information about the workings of government" (p. 7). These citizens' new attitudes were one impetus that incited a reexamination of archival theory and the nature of records beginning in the 1980s. Increased demands for different kinds of information have led archivists to reconsider how that information is saved and what it means to save information. Heald (1996) ties the increased interest in archival documentation to changing expectations of citizens in regards to their governments. As governmental accountability and transparency become more popular, archival documentation does as well. The recontextualization of the archive through the postmodern paradigm expands the business of the archive into both an official, governmental, and cultural mandate. Cook (2001) notes that the archive, in the postmodern paradigm, changes purpose from an exclusively statist, power-based structure to a collective, memory-based structure.

The implications of this shift can be found in every aspect of archival work, but are very apparent in appraisal theory. Finally, working with newly defined records and archives can prove challenging, such that new appraisal methods need to be employed in order for archivists to work with records that come in varied formats, are dynamic, and possibly unprecedented in archival history. Such drastic changes have happened quickly in the archival world in terms of content, media, and volatility of records. The contemporary paradigm seeks to understand the archive through a different framework than past paradigms. With change as the only constant, the contemporary archival paradigm seeks to remain vital to the creation of history and memory.

Many Archivists, Many Questions

Previous archival paradigms have changed as a result of one person's or an established group of authors' work with specific sets of records. While the types of records the five archivists discussed here concern themselves with are indeed different from the records of past archival paradigms, the one characteristic that binds the records together is their differences in terms of content, use, and even format. The same binding difference is true for the geographic locations of each of the archivists' work environments. The archival paradigms described above can be linked to geography: the Dutch consolidation of many archives in the Netherlands, Jenkinson's British war records from World War I, and Schellenberg's records from the United States during the postwar era. In contrast to previous paradigms, archivists all over the world have simultaneously worked to create the most contemporary Questioning archival paradigm. The five archivists discussed here work in Canada, the United States, and the Netherlands. The records these archivists work with are in various formats, including paper and electronic, and share the common trait of being dispersed in every direction along a field of content and context.

Much like the wide variety formats found in contemporary archives, the archivists discussed below are brought together here for the first time to form a single archival paradigm. This group of archivists is constructed differently from the archivists who created past archival paradigms in that they are currently active in the field, working in separate archives and situations, and have not necessarily intentionally sought to create a new archival paradigm as a group. The Questioning archival paradigm continues to be created and re-created by this group of archivists along with others who contribute to the growing discourse on archival theory.

One of the motivations for these archivists to question archival theory is the increased emphasis on diversity in many realms including the work of historians, demands from archive users, and institutional and governmental needs. While diversity continues to play a key role in contemporary archives, many of the theorists cited here are white and male. The distinct lack of archival theories from varied points of view is a hindrance to a full and well-informed perspective. Unfortunately, a healthy diversity is not to be found in the ranks of archival theorists. That is, not yet. As the Society of American Archivists continues to stress the importance of diversity within that organization and more people from diverse backgrounds are trained as archivists and begin to question archival paradigms, a lack of diversity will be less of an issue. This paragraph is also not intended to absolve either the author or reader of responsibility of seeking out diverse points of view with regard to archival theory. However, without acknowledgment of a lack of diversity, the contemporary profession and this writing would ring untrue. Diversity is a specific instance of the type of self-reflexive questioning that is at the heart of the most contemporary of archival paradigms.

The specific archivists working to create the archival paradigm include Brien Brothman, who is a link between the United States and Canada and represents the North American theoretical perspective in both his archival and academic work. After earning a doctorate in history from Université Laval in Quebec City, Brothman worked at the National Archives Canada, specializing in the documentation of government science and technology programs. He has also held a position at the Rhode Island State Archives.

Brothman is currently an adjunct professor of European History at Bristol College in Massachusetts.

Where other archival theorists have approached the work of appraisal theory through a mixture of theoretical writing and practical application, Brothman has focused on archival and appraisal theories influenced by postmodern and poststructuralist philosophies. According to the International Conference on the History of Records and Archives (2005), Brothman "has had a longstanding interest in philosophical and historical perspectives on information technology and archival practice, with a particular focus on deconstructive writing and textual production" (para. 1). Brothman's research interests are within the contemporary archival paradigm that views archives as a means of communication and capable of being interpreted as such. His academic writing has reflected the contemporary paradigm and focuses on theoretical and philosophical approaches to archival discourse.

Carolyn Heald has worked as an archivist and records consultant in both governmental and university settings in Canada. Heald earned a master's degree in history from Queen's University in Kingston, Ontario, Canada and a master's degree in library science from the University of Toronto. During her studies at Queen's University, Heald won the *Canadian Library Journal's* student paper award and was published in the journal in 1992.

Heald has continued to publish articles about postmodern critical thought and archives in archival journals including *American Archivist* and *Archivaria*. She worked as a Senior Archivist in the Health/Social Portfolio at the Archives of Ontario, Toronto beginning in 1990. More recently, she has been appointed to a position as the Director of the Information and Privacy Office at York University in Toronto.

Heather MacNeil has been very active in teaching and publishing about archives and archival theory since 1999. She two master's degrees, one in English, from Simon Fraser University in Burnaby, British Columbia, and another in archival science, from the University of British Columbia. MacNeil earned a Ph. D. in Interdisciplinary Studies, which includes the study of law, history, and archival science, also from the University of British Columbia.

MacNeil currently teaches at the University of British Columbia's School of Library, Archival, and Information Studies, where she has been on the faculty since 1999 ("Faculty of Information Studies," 2007). She has published five books and numerous articles concerning archives and archival theory including topics as broad-ranging as archival arrangement and description, authenticity of archival records, interdisciplinary definitions of archival records, and the preservation of electronic records. MacNeil currently serves on Editorial Board of *Archivaria* and the Publications Board of the Society of American Archivists ("Faculty of Information Studies," 2007).

Working from the Netherlands, the home country of Muller, Feith, and Fruin, Eric Ketelaar has published over 250 articles concerned with archives in Dutch, English, French, and German. Trained as a lawyer and having earned his law degree in 1967 from Leiden University and a doctorate in law, also from Leiden, Ketelaar began his career as an archivist after school. From 1980 to 1984, he served as the Secretary for Standardization of the International Council on Archives. Subsequently, Ketelaar worked as the Secretary of the International Conference of the Round Table on Archives from 1984 to 1992. During this time, he began his professional career with the state archives of the Netherlands, serving as Deputy General State Archivist from 1980 to 1984, State Archivist of Groningen from 1984 to 1989, and State Archivist of the Netherlands from 1989 to 1997. In 2000, he was appointed Honorary President of the International Council on Archives (Ketelaar, 2006).

Ketelaar has also been very active in professional organizations in the Netherlands. He has served the Royal Society of Dutch Archivists as Vice President and President, and was Chairman of the Steering Committee on Automation. In 1987 the Society awarded him with the first Hendrik van Wijn medal for his work as editor of the series of thirteen guides to the archival repositories in the Netherlands.

The most well known and prolific of the archivists working within the new appraisal paradigm is Terry Cook. Cook has worked with the Canadian national archives for a majority of his professional life, specializing in appraisal for over 20 years. In 1998, he left the National Archives Canada as a senior manager, where he directed "the appraisal and records disposition programme," (ICHORA-2 2005). He holds a Ph.D. in Canadian history from Queen's University in Kingston, Ontario. Cook has published widely in the profession, with more than 80 publications on archival subjects, including the *Archival Appraisal of Records Containing Personal Information: A RAMP Study With Guidelines* in 1991, co-editing *Imagining Archives: Essays and Reflections by Hugh A. Taylor* in 2003, and his latest book, *Electronic Records Practice: Lessons from the National Archives of Canada* in 2005.

Cook has also served as the past editor of *Archivaria*, two Canadian studies series, and the Canadian Historical Association's *Journal*. In 2002, he also co-edited four issues of the journal *Archival Science* which focused on archives, records, and power. He is a past fellow of the Society of American Archivists as well as a visiting professor in the Master's Programme in Archival Studies at the University of Manitoba. He has also taught at the Universities of Michigan, Maryland, and Monash University in Australia.

Questioning the Past

Interpretation answers and asks some questions and asks others

Archivists working within the Questioning paradigm have conceived of archival theory as a theory of communication. The transmission of information from archival document to user, from *fonds* to archivist, from record creator to an active document, are all examples of areas in which communication takes place in the archival context. Within each step of communication lies the possibility for interpretation between transmission and reception of information. A theoretical basis that these contemporary archivists have adopted and that explicitly concentrates on this communication/interpretation discourse is postmodern critical thought.

Beyond communication and interpretation, a basic concept in postmodern critical theory, is the notion that communication is based on the interpretation of signs. This point of view creates a system in which representation becomes equally, if not more, important than the content carried by signs. As a whole, the system created results in a semiotics of interpretation that displaces metanarrative. According to Lyotard (1979/1984), metanarrative is the grand narratives of progress, especially in the study of history, which no longer represent the contemporary understanding of history. In Lyotard's approach, causal relationships in historical narratives are viewed as constructed, rather than inherently true, and interpretation is required to understand and create meaning. This is an approach to history that is literary in nature, that, when combined with the concepts of the "linguistic turn," in the writing of history, creates a very different historical narrative than that of the historical paradigm that is based on causal relationships.

Much of the paradigm shift to contemporary appraisal theory is based upon the notion that the archive contains socially created information about people, both individuals and groups. One definition of social information is, "a set of mental, coded, and socially contextualized representations (significant symbols) possible of being recorded on any medium (paper, film, magnetic tape, etc.) and, therefore, permanently communicated" (Ribeiro, 2001, p. 304-5). Interpretation in the contemporary archive creates further complexity through increased subjectivity not only in appraisal, but in all aspects of archival work. In the writing of the five archivists discussed here, it is clear that the appraisal of records for the contemporary archive has shifted to accommodate a new paradigm based on the archive as a means of communication. A significant component of this new understanding of the archive as communication is interpretation and recontextualization. Within the contemporary archival paradigm, records and the archive itself are subject to the uncertainty brought with communication and interpretation, a far cry from the notions of objectivity favored in telling history "as it happened."

Brothman's approach to the new archival paradigm is to encourage further contemplation of the cultural meaning of contemporary archival practice and to initiate reflection on the social role that archives play in society. The self-reflexive questioning required for this type of introspection is inherited from postmodern critical thought, which examines assumptions and questions notions of naturalness. These questions seek to create "a reflexive examination of the social and historical meaning of the terms of archival engagement" (Brothman, 1991, p. 80). The contemporary archival paradigm is perhaps the first time a paradigm shift has taken place in which the archivists are fully aware of the intention to change the paradigm itself and have defined their intentions in those terms. Jenkinson staunchly defended his "archives of the future" from the vagaries of subjectivity in the form of appraisal and Schellenberg effectively transformed North American archival practice, but neither mention operating in respect to archival theory self-consciously.

Schellenberg's paradigm shift is invoked in Brothman's assessment of the role technology plays in interpretation. He argues that changes in communication technology should compel archivists to reassess the meaning of the profession's most secure principles. Electronic records have challenged archivists' definitions of records while capable advanced reproduction methods have brought the notion of originality into question, as well. Elizabeth Eisenstein, as cited by Brothman (1991), a printing and communication technology scholar, notes that communication technology is important to historic consciousness and becomes an important part of the context of communication.

Brothman (1991) undertakes the reevaluation of archival concepts and understanding archives through the lens of poetics. This approach contains a new vocabulary for archivists to use in understanding their profession. The use of poetics is part of the linguistic turn in the archival profession, one that holds poetics in equal esteem with a scientific approach. The results of Brothman's reevaluation delineates between two bases of practice: cultural and administrative. The former draws from literary, philosophical, and historiographic sources to create archival criteria based an interdisciplinary milieu. The latter consists of more traditional archival practices that focus on maintaining records of action taken by a group, organization, government, or company. For Brothman, the increasingly imperceptible boundary between information managers and archivists portends a shift in focus from cultural practice to administrative practice, with the latter possibly fatal to archives as a cultural discipline (p. 78). The warning is that if archivists ignore the cultural mandate of their profession, in favor of an administrative point of view and role, the profession will lose its vitality follows this assessment. As Brothman (1991) states, "For archivists to abstain from cultural awareness and criticism is tantamount to professional irresponsibility" (p. 90).

Critical theory and the archive

The definition of postmodern critical thought is historically and perhaps intentionally diffuse and vague. Postmodern critical thought values plurality and questioning which can lead to new concepts or contentious argument, and often times, both. While each attempt at a singular definition can be met with equally coherent and possible counter argument, Fredric Jameson's definition, as cited by Heald (1996), is interesting and useful, "It is safest to grasp the concept of the postmodern as an attempt to think historically in an age that has forgotten how to think historically in the first place" (p. 89). The archivists who work within the questioning paradigm have attempted to link their contemporary work with archivists of the past while problematizing the assumptions previous archivists took for granted. The result is an intellectualized and subjective approach to a formerly practical and objective point of view. Cook (2001) observes that postmodernism's diversity of meanings produces difficulty in the creation of a linear definition. Instead of a linear definition, a somewhat sprawling, interdisciplinary, and anecdote-filled attempt at explanation will have to suffice, as even the foremost theorists do not agree that a single definition of postmodern critical thought is possible or desirable.

One component of a definition that postmodern thinkers have employed to reconcile postmodern theory with the contemporary situation as presented in late capitalism is the notion that signs have surpassed the actions or realities they represent. Jean Baudrillard is one of the most emphatic opponents of the significance of signs in postmodern thought, and notes that the unnecessary significance of signs, communication, and information is linked to the obsession with finding causes, origins and the obliteration of finalities (Brothman, 1991). An example of Baudrillard's protestations in terms of archival theory can be found in the assignation of records to signify action taken by the record creator. In this example, Baudrillard's argument would deemphasize this importance of the record as it has, in its function as a report of action, become a sign for that action. Archivists whose approach is informed by postmodern critical theory are presented with a need to redefine the notion of an archival record if it is understood to be a sign wrought with possibilities for varied interpretations and different understandings. The definition of the archival record is one gap in knowledge exposed in the Questioning archival paradigm.

Questions of Records and Archives

The contemporary archival paradigm, more than any previous paradigm, is based on an assessment of past archival theories. The archivists who work within the Questioning paradigm then analyze these assessments and new theories are created in combination with contemporary archival needs. Examples of these questions can be found around issues like *respect des fonds*, the role of the archivist, and the discourse between objectivity and subjectivity in the archive. The contemporary archival paradigm has sought to question the assumptions and knowledge of past archival theory and to define new archival theories based upon the possible answers to those questions. These tactics are in direct contrast to those of previous archival paradigms that were established and created to fill a governmental need in terms of archival organization. Another characteristic that is not shared between the Questioning paradigm and preceding paradigms is an indelible belief in objectivity as a steadfast assumption within archival theory.

Past archival paradigms have been, in part, based upon the notion that the accumulation of records is a natural process and that archives are the natural result of such action. Schwartz and Cook (2002) question this precept when they note that current archival practice is based upon tradition and this belief in the "naturalness" of records which are, as a means of communication, socially created. In a separate article, Cook and Schwartz (2002) elaborate on this theme and note that Judith Butler's naturalization of practice, in this case archivists who remain determined to base their theories on historical paradigms, creates a situation in which an expectation of practice is met through carrying out activities that will fulfill the expectation. The concept is that stagnant theory will produce stagnant practice, a tautology. Butler goes on to note that the fulfillment of theoretical expectations becomes normalized through repetition. In this case, while the archival paradigm shifts, archivists outside of the Questioning paradigm can reassure themselves that established theory creates desirable results because these results are what they have been trained to expect.

Changes in the users of archives also have an impact upon the definition of the archive and its records. As personal identity comes to the fore in terms of individuals' political affinities and social interactions, it becomes important for the interpretation of records in the archive. Schwartz and Cook (2002) discuss identity as a basis for theory in two terms, intrinsic and social. Intrinsic identity can be associated with past archival paradigms in which records and the archive as a whole are associated with realness and concrete truth. A social definition of identity and records is associated with constructedness and external reasons for creation. One of the important aspects of the application of postmodern critical thought to archival theory is the questioning of archival assumptions and definitions. While a postmodern definition of a record may be less than straightforward, the constructive criticism of past definitions can illuminate possibilities for change. Postmodern thought has been criticized for being relativistic and without moral value, but its questioning of the definition of records and archives is the key to representation in the archive of diverse groups of people. Heald (1996) explains "For in the postmodern husk of moral relativism and epistemological skepticism is a kernel of social tolerance. In this world of fragmented and decontextualized information, we can now have a multiplicity of histories" (p. 96).

Postmodernism in archival theory is the equivalent to the linguistic turn in the writing of history. In order for archivists to achieve a parallel paradigm shift, the profession can undertake what Butler, as cited by Cook and Schwartz (2002), refers to as a trangressive performance, as a means to go beyond the current practice to create something new with different value. Three ways archivists can achieve a transgressive performance as a profession are: first, question tacit narratives that have guided archival work for at least the past 110 years; second, deliver more nuanced performance in terms of records, and theories which are expected by users; and third, begin to understand that new views in society demand new approaches in the archive, There is a disconnect between archivists who have yet to take action on the social revolutions of the 1960s and 1970s and contemporary demands placed, upon and expectations of, the archive.

New demands of the archive from both citizens and governments include increased transparency, especially in appraisal theory. Transparency is both mandated by archive users and postmodern archival theory, as proper appraisal requires an understanding of the society in which the records were created. MacNeil (1994) illustrates this point when she explains: "What has changed in a postmodern context is making the implicit explicit; an increase in transparency" (p. 9). In the postmodern archival paradigm, questioning has lead to the need for openness and increased oversight by multiple groups of people, including users of the archive.

The desire for transparency is itself an outgrowth of the Enlightenment-based ideal of true history. Archive users, especially historians, need to trust that archival records do indeed contain the truth. In the past, this has been implicitly guaranteed by a record's inclusion in the archive. This is especially important for historians who write fact-based history, which posits causal relationships over time. The postmodern paradigm, in both the writing of history and archives, is less about causes and more focused on points of view, communication, and interpretation. Unfortunately, archivists can only work with records that are presented to them for inclusion in the archive. Postmodern theory questions the reliability of archival records not to spin the archive and writing of history into chaos, but in order to begin to understand more about the assumptions archivists make about their work.

If postmodern critical thought is a difficult proposition for an archival paradigm shift, the concepts that surround a postmodern interpretation of the value in records themselves is even more difficult. As the record is the smallest unit of organization in the archive, it is the basis for all archival work and theory; its place and understanding its meanings are important. Cook and Schwartz (2002, p. 178) are clearly supportive of a new definition: "records emerging from the creation process are anything but natural, organic, innocent residues of disinterested administrative transactions. Rather they are value-laden instruments of power." The new definition of value-laden instruments of power accounts for the uses of records and takes their evidentiary nature for granted by recognizing that power is derived from the records themselves. Ketelaar (2002) adds perspective to the discussion of records and power when he notes that power is created through the use and interpretation of records, that records themselves have no power, but become the tools of power through interpretation and re-contextualization.

Schwartz and Cook (2002) discuss the fact that most users of archives assume that archival records are issue-free and unproblematic sources of straightforward historical facts. The concepts of context, original order, and *respect des fonds* have been a part of archival theory to protect records' information, but cannot compensate for the questioning of power involved in the declarative statement of truth placed upon a record by either archivists or archive users. The records themselves have no opinion regarding their own value, it is interpretation of the record by an archivist that creates value for users.

In the Questioning archival paradigm, the newly discovered power in the interpretation of records creates a powerful dynamic between the record and the archivist. Craig, as quoted by Cook and Schwartz (2002), notes this: "record keeping is as much about interpretation and communication dynamics as about 'rule-guided systems for information artifacts" (p. 177). The dynamic relationship between archivist, archival user, and information in records as expressed through interpretation changes the connection archivists have to records. The relationship becomes one of engagement, especially in contrast to a disinterested keeper of records. Once this connection is modified, the value perceived in records, the main source of information considered during appraisal, changes. As Brothman (1991) argues, these changes affect the whole continuum of archival information: "The history of the record does not stop at the portals of archives. Archives are participants in that history" (p. 91).

Questioning the concept of the record is intended as a means to assess the knowledge that surrounds concepts of the record and its context. One of these gaps is the inability to understand records in an ahistorical manner, outside of a contemporary context. Ketelaar (2001) explains this conundrum as the contemporary use of records retrospectively affects the outlook on other records. It is much easier to recognize contemporary interpretation of records, not just new records. Heald (1996) builds on this notion of immediacy in the definition of records' worth by noting that the social understanding of archives is based upon the idea that records themselves do not change, rather, the interpretations of records change in different contexts.

As historians have continued to transform the uses of records in research, texts have become primary rather than secondary sources. The result is that archivists and historians alike have questioned established concepts of archival records. (Brothman, 1991). These questions, according to Schwartz and Cook (2002), stem from a collective memory approach and include: "who is doing the documenting, what are the impact of changes in theory on records management and archival practice?" p. 5). These questions map to Foucault's (1972) post-structuralist questioning of knowledge, designed to illuminate gaps in knowledge: "Who is speaking (who has the right to speak and why?); what are the sites from which the discourse emanates? (physical and metaphysical); what are the positions of the subject in relation to the various domains or groups of objects?" (p. 50). Ketelaar (2002) specifically discusses the need to question and recognize the fallibility in records and adds that the assumed reality of the archive can and should be questioned.

As evidence of action, archival records have been placed on a theoretical pedestal, previously exempt from changes in theory. The contemporary archival paradigm recognizes the power of records and evidence, but also seeks to problematize that power. An illustration of this is Ketelaar's concept of double power. Depending on the point of view of the user, the power of records can be freeing or damning. The evidence in a record can liberate the oppressed or be interpreted as a means of further repression. Records can also illustrate evidence of oppression and the means through which past oppression can be corrected (Ketelaar, 2002). Since records contain information that is released through interpretation, there are always many possibilities for many uses of records.

The contemporary archival paradigm is the first to self-consciously question many of the assumptions of past archival theories and interpretations of meanings within the archival context. While other theories focus on specific situations and create new archival paradigms based on completed work, the postmodern archival paradigm seeks to initiate change from the inside out. Rather than a linear, progressive approach, the contemporary archival paradigm is circular, self-reflexive, and multi-dimensional, calling the notion of progress in archival theory and its benefits into question in the process.

Rather than seek guidance from within the profession, the contemporary paradigm draws its orientation from critical theory and academia. Theorists such as Foucault and Derrida understand the archive to be a metaphorical construct, a place to discuss human knowledge, memory, power, and justice (Schwartz & Cook, 2002). The contemporary paradigm posits that the lack of theoretical evaluation of key archival concepts can prove problematic in the long term. Without acute theoretical awareness, archivists who work exclusively and unquestioningly within any paradigm risk missing the opportunity to be innovative in exchange for inherited theory and practice.

An example of inherited practice questioned in the contemporary paradigm is the concept of *respect des fonds*. MacNeil (1994) criticizes the concept as a kind of unnecessary archival specificity in that it represents a type of knowledge that does not exist in the same form in any other organizational scheme. MacNeil criticizes this concept, one that is central to previous archival paradigms. In this postmodern critical point of view, however, the principles of *respects des fonds* are: interrelatedness as to meaning, authenticity as to procedure, and impartiality as to creation. For some archival theorists, these principles are circumstantial guarantees of reliability in terms of evidence. MacNeil proposes a restatement of *respect des fonds* in a contemporary archival context, one that "involves the separating out of the various contexts of documents' creation in order to better reveal their relation to one another" (MacNeil, 1994, p. 9). Whether this is a physical or intellectual separation is unspecified. The challenge to inherited practice remains a consistently present motivation for reevaluation of basic archival concepts.

The contemporary archival paradigm is one that is historically oriented and engaged with questioning many, if not all, concepts and values that may have been taken for granted in past archival theories and paradigms. The most recent paradigm shift includes questioning core concepts to better understand archival theory as a whole. While the archival paradigm continues to shift, archivists have begun to look beyond the self-evident justification of practice to create a self-conscious and self-reflexive archival paradigm inclusive of well-crafted theory. This new paradigm is most easily recognizable in the acceptance of increased subjectivity in appraisal theory.

Perhaps the most well-known contemporary appraisal theory that seeks to combine practice and allow for increased subjectivity in archival theory for mutual benefit is Terry Cook's Macroappraisal. Cook (2000) describes Macroappraisal as a way to enact postmodern theory directly in appraisal work, a way to combine theory and practice to create *praxis*. In Macroappraisal, the criteria for records appraisal is based upon the functions of entities and the relationships between those entities rather than the records those entities produced. It is a very postmodern approach that attempts to comprehend archival work through understanding the power structures upon which entities are created. The idea is that the expressions of an entity's work, its archival records, are ultimately expressed in the same groupings and divisions as the organization of the entity itself. Macroappraisal is an manifestation of the effectiveness of a combination of theory and practice.

Brothman's (1991) combination of theory and practice is based on the notion that appraisal theory is necessary for responsible archivists who seek to select viable records that represent the entity's evidence. This theory is based on the notion that archives, at the core, are about physical and intellectual order. Appraisal is a part of the ordering of archives, as it helps to ensure records are kept in their proper place. Since the proper place is created through first creating an intellectual space to be proper in, appraisal creates value through negative space. Records in the archive become more valuable than discarded records by virtue of other records no longer in existence. Weeding activities do take place after a shift in values, but for the most part, once records have entered the archive, their value is permanently maintained.

Possible Answers: The Role of the Archivist

The role of the archivist has changed significantly over time. From Jenkinson's passive keeper of records, to Schellenberg's administrative records manager, and now, in the contemporary paradigm, to the active, intellectually engaged, and challenging creator and custodian of cultural memory, the role of the archivist has shifted from being exclusively administrative to encompassing a broad range of mandates from administration to cultural selector and curator. Through expanding and modifying the role the archivist plays in the archive, the contemporary paradigm has sought to broaden the intellectual engagement of archivists in their work. Increased intellectual engagement can create a significant role in the sometimes contentious world of helping to create identity through archival records. Schwartz and Cook (2002) note:

> "Whether conscious of it or no, archivists are major players in the business of identity politics. Archivists appraise, collect, and preserve the props with which notions of identity are built. In turn, notions of identity are confirmed and justified as historical documents validate with all their authority as "evidence" the identity stories so built" (p. 16).

Because archivists work with materials that are designated as official evidence, the type of information contained in records can either be used to refute power or enforce it. As Ketelaar argues, sometimes records can do both. The power of proof is still subject to interpretation.

Heald (1996) prescribes an understanding of the form and function of documentary records to the new role of the archivist. These notions of form and function create a new, circumspect view of the power of records. Cook and Schwartz (2002) describe the contemporary role of the archivist: "Above all [postmodern theory] asserts that no actor or observer, historian or archivist, is ever neutral or disinterested in any documentary process, nor is any 'text' they consult (including archival documents) or preserve ... a transparent window to some past reality" (p. 182). They call into question many aspects of the documentary process, from creation of records to archiving, to use in historical writing. To question the very theoretical basis of archival theory is a radical departure from every previous archival paradigm. Preceding paradigms were established upon the notion that the newly formed paradigm was an extension of the previous paradigms' concepts. The contemporary paradigm seeks to make a significant break from this lineage. In an attempt to dismantle metanarratives regarding the role of the archivist, the hidden and assumed categorization, codification, and labeling of archives and archivists has come into question (Ketelaar, 2001). Seeking to question previous paradigms' assumptions, though radical in its results, is somewhat reactionary since it is based on previous paradigm's concerns and reactions.

The contemporary archivist, according to Cook (2001), participates in the creation of meaning through the creation of context and replication of narratives. This includes the passage of past archival techniques, but with a new, more self-reflexive and simultaneously active role for the archivist. Cook explains further that the replication of narrative is very distinct from the protection of evidence, in that the replication of narrative is valued by a cultural mandate while the protection of evidence is traditionally based in a legal need. The issue for the new role of the archivist in the postmodern archival paradigm is the separation of the archival culture of the past and the mandate to protect evidence of action. MacNeil (1994) suggests that archivists can fulfill a more cultural mandate through a new analysis of structures, functions, and competencies associated with activities to appraise and describe archival documents well.

The first step toward a new professional stature for the archivist, according to Cook and Schwartz (2002), is to recognize and celebrate the role of the archivist as valuable, a role that is proud of the impact archivists have on the archive and its information and does not attempt to keep the archivist's role hidden from users or the outside world. Cook (2001) explains that the new role for the archivist goes beyond public recognition of the contributions archivists make to the cultural record. The new role is informed, in part, by a new understanding of records as dynamic, archivists with an active point of view of their work rather than passive guardians, and, in general, a move to active verbs rather than static practices. This means that the discussion of archives changes from "archives" to "archiving," for instance.

The role of the archivist has never changed as quickly or as radically as those archivists who work within the Questioning paradigm propose in their writing. From the passive keeper of records to a modern records manager, and now, to a culturally engaged creator of public memory, the role of the archivist can be defined as malleable within certain bounds over the past 100 years. The archivist, as a functionary of a larger organization, is always at least partially beholden to the organization's interest. In this situation, the archivist must always attempt to please the needs of his or her contemporaries with the records of the past. One of the main guiding forces behind the changing role of the archivist is the dialectic between objectivity and subjectivity in archival theory. As cultural and social expectations of archives change over time, so to does the role archivists play in creating and maintaining the adaptable archives.

Objectivity Is A Matter Of Interpretation

The tension between subjectivity and objectivity in archival appraisal has been present since Muller, Feith, and Fruin first established a coherent archival paradigm in which they created an archival ideal and described how to achieve that goal. This tension is brought to the forefront in the contemporary archival paradigm. The result of inquiries into the history of appraisal theory, according to Heald, is a strained power dynamic between archivists who believe in a more subjective approach to archiving and those who prefer more traditional theories based on objectivity. Cook and Schwartz (2002) find themselves firmly in the former group of archivists when they remark: "Put simply, what archives keep and what archives do is socially grounded in time and space" (p. 184). The questions regarding archival theory's attempts to create truthful evidence from records of the past begins to bring time-honored theoretical constructs into question: "Archival science exhibits a similar desire to extract some kind of objective unadulterated record of the past. Such propensities raise questions about original order (and *respect des fonds*)" (Brothman, 1991, p. 83). These questions are partially answered within the creation of the contemporary archival paradigm and its associated questioning of records and the role of the archivist. As a result, the future of archives will be in new and different directions.

One of these new directions is a movement from an exclusively administrative to a combined cultural mandate. The result of this shift is a new view of the archive, one that embraces subjectivity in appraisal and relies more upon the individual archivist's approach to archiving. Archival paradigms of the past have dictated that archivists assume records were created as impartial products of a business or organization's work. The contemporary appraisal paradigm questions the infallibility of not only records, but also the records' creators. MacNeil (1994) argues that impartiality is not present in the creation of records since the ideas contained in the records are themselves interpretations. Archivists have been dedicated, then, to preserving the biases of subjective records over time. MacNeil (1994) also points out that this is a point at which subjectivity becomes even more problematic as there have been major disagreements between archival problems of the past and current concerns in archival theory especially in terms of "how to limit and control the distortion of the documentary heritage that is caused by the subjective process of apportioning value to documents" (p. 12). The archivists who seek to change the archival paradigm must determine which is the lesser of two evils, subjective appraisal or the continuation of subjective decision-making by records creators.

It is again useful to recall that cultural theorists such as Derrida have many questions of the archive and have an interest in archivists' responses. For these critics the archive represents, among other things, the totality of state power and or the exclusion of non-sanctioned, ex-centric voices and narratives, while for archivists these are not only fairly new questions, but also new perspectives on their own theoretical orientation. For these critics to question the hierarchy of value in a strictly objective archival paradigm is to acknowledge that documents are kept in the archive by virtue of a topology of privilege, a space where unique information and law intersect in a result of privilege (Derrida, 1995). Social power and privilege can be used to reinforce political power, thereby creating a situation ripe for hegemony and the possible legal silencing of underrepresented people. Ketelaar (2002) expands on this notion of unbridled power based upon the notion of archival objectivity when he notes that legal rights guaranteed by the supposed objectivity of archival records translate into privilege in the archive. Thus, rather than alleviating the tension between subjective and objective points of view, the contemporary paradigm increases these tensions through its questioning of both information and governmental power.

Archivists who work within the contemporary paradigm argue that while past theories may have been appropriate products of a specific time and place, these contexts have changed while the theory involved with the archives has not caught up to every contemporary context. Ketelaar (2001) specifically addresses the role appraisal plays in the creation of value. He states that societies cannot remember everything, and therefore, cultural memory is created through forgetting, through the negative space in social memory. The contemporary appraisal paradigm accepts this forgetfulness as part of the archival wager. It seeks to reconcile its shortcomings in an effort to create a self-reflexive theory that is malleable enough to allow for changes while it remains responsive to users and archivists' needs. One example of the contemporary paradigm's self-reflexive theoretical litheness is Brothman's (1991) assessment that, through appraisal processes, original order is already broken and therefore does not necessarily constitute the only organization scheme for an archive.

Questioning original order specifically addresses a major issue in appraisal theory: how to justify the selection of specific records while maintaining the integrity of the *fonds* as a whole? One theory is Brothman's (1991) notion that the ordering of archival information is socially constructed. This construction includes the hierarchy of value given to original order and the naturalness of pre-appraisal records. Brothman's argument is indeed very postmodern, one that eschews the notion of linear progress, in this case, of information, toward a specific goal of logical organization. This view is that information is essentially random and does not inherently progress toward any goal. Rather, information exists in the world and is manipulated by individuals, including archivists, to specific ends. Actions such as appraisal give value to information because of appraisal's transformative power. Records in archives become valuable because they begin as information and, in part through the appraisal process, become archival records.

The postmodern treatment of records becomes, as Heald (1996) terms it, "records as narrative sources of context" (p. 93). If records shift from evidence of action taken to Heald's sources of context, their appraisal status can also change. The notions of original order and subjectivity in appraisal can drastically change with a contemporary point of view. Heald describes appraisal as an important part of the archival process. The focus becomes the process by which records become archives, not whether or not an objective answer is found. To postmodern archivists, the right answer may never be found, since a correct answer would denote the end of the search. Instead, archivists working in the contemporary paradigm acknowledge Derrida's claim that the structure of the archive determines what will be in the archive. As Derrida (1995) notes: "The archivization produces as much as records the event" (p. 16-17). Contrary previous archival paradigms, the postmodern archivist actually increases the value of records by undertaking appraisal activities rather than devaluing records that are not saved.

The proposal put forward by postmodern archivists, that they allow more subjective criteria to become part of appraisal activities, is a radical one. To acknowledge less than a striving cumulative progress toward objectivity in archival work is to work against the tide of the history of archival appraisal theory. Heald (1996) finds a reexamination of appraisal theory invigorating for the profession. These archivists answer their own questions with further questions: Perhaps a radical reunderstanding and reimagining of the archive is what is needed? Perhaps all archival theory should be about archives, not the organizations' records within the archive? Derrida (1995) lays down the gauntlet more forcefully: "the limits, the borders and the distinctions have been shaken by an earthquake from which no classificational concept and no implementation of the archive can be sheltered. Order is no longer assured" (p. 5).

Postmodern critical theory has given new possibilities to archivists in which they can begin to self-consciously understand the assumptions and processes that have been taken for granted in past archival paradigms. It illustrates how archives have power over "the administrative, legal, and fiscal accountability of governments, corporations, and individuals and engage in powerful public policy debates around the right to know, freedom of information, protection of privacy, copyright and intellectual property" (Schwartz & Cook, 2002, p. 2). The shift from citizens accountable to government to government accountable to citizens has been made possible through the existence of archival information. The contemporary archival paradigm seeks to create a dynamic theory that can continue to remain at the vanguard of the creation of cultural and administrative memory.

Through the honest assessment of points of power, including governments, archivists who have engaged with postmodern thought and critical points of view have begun to understand the power dynamic in archives in a new way. Postmodern critical thought disperses power through a flattening of hierarchies. This is recognition that, regardless of social status, each individual's truth is incomplete. MacNeil (1994) reframes the criticism into a discussion of tolerance within archival theory. She notes that an open mind is important for archivists as "the truthfulness of our truths ... is necessarily constrained by the limitations of our individual perspectives; our truths are, at best, partial ones" (p.18). If postmodern critical theory in an archival perspective has allowed for different individuals to be represented in the historical record through tolerance of varied perspectives, it has also allowed for the multiplication of perspectives as Ketelaar (2001) describes. Postmodern critical theory opens archival theory to new and varied possibilities rather than merely relativizing the truth.

This dynamic theory includes the recognition of the power of the archive, which, according to Schwartz and Cook (2002), is, itself, about maintaining power: the power of the present to know what is and will be known about the past, and the power of remembering over forgetting. Power plays an important role in the creation of memory from archives as well as guiding archivists in their appraisal decisions. Both appraisal and deaccessioning are key power points in the records continuum. It is at these points that contemporary archivists have concentrated their theoretical efforts as both the most evident and the most accessible for archivists and theorists alike.

Records themselves continue to be a point of power for governments, citizens, organizations, and archivists as the need for individuals to have access to evidence in the form of documentary records for proof of action taken. Heald (1996) discusses the increased need for the documentary record as part of the success of democracy, and notes that documents are needed more than ever because society itself has deemed them valuable. This guarantee is especially well suited for the United States which holds states' rights in high regard as it allows for local development of values. Brothman (1991) locates the creation of value as community-based. Postmodern archival theory includes this flexibility for standards from location to location or even agency to agency. In fact, this flexibility recognizes what has been in place for quite sometime: that archivists make their appraisal decisions based on more narrow, sometimes even personal, criteria rather than a strict set of universal and objective rules shared within the profession.

The criticism from postmodern critics that is leveled at archival and appraisal theory is done with positive intentions. Schwartz and Cook (2002) note that the goals of a postmodern consideration of the archive are to understand more about the power/knowledge nexus, the relationship between representation and reality, history and memory, place and identity, and to comprehend the specificity of the relationship between archival practice and societal needs. Since much work in the Questioning paradigm comes from within the framework of criticism, the results can be difficult for practicing archivists to accept without feelings of defensiveness or even frustration. This is not the intent of this archival paradigm, however. Brothman (1991) argues that the *tone* of these critiques is important, as there should be no implicit or explicit disapproval of current archival practice. There should be analysis and description, and, instead of prescription, interpretation.

The Final Question

If there is a result of the self-conscious investigations made by the archivists discussed here regarding appraisal theory in a postmodern context, it is that the shift of the archival paradigm in terms of professional issues and issues of cultural memory will be an ongoing discourse within the profession. Whether this discourse is expressed through new archival theories, structures, concepts, or a continuum, the result of these investigations is that answers are being continually defined. Some theorists such as Ketelaar (2001) suggest new conceptions of archival structure that allow for the infusion of values that are embedded in each and every activation of the archive. Others, like Terry Cook, suggest new strategies and re-conceptions of appraisal activities with an eye toward understanding the interactions between citizens and governments.

Regardless of which path an individual archivist follows relative to the level of objectivity in his or her own theory and practice, the question of the archive itself constantly looms large. Perhaps postmodern critical theory is the theoretical framework of the current archival paradigm because there is no definitive answer for what archivists, citizens, or historians want from the archive. Derrida (1991, p. 33) says it best:

> Do we *already* have at our disposition a concept of the archive? . . . Which is one and whose unity is deserved? Have we ever been assured of the homogeneity, of the consistency, of the univocal relationship of any concept to a term or to such a word as "archive?" (italics in original)

From the results of the analysis above, the answer is a resounding "No." This lack of unity is not, however, negative for the archival profession or for archival theory. The willingness to acknowledge the lack of a definitive answer to Derrida's question underscores a level of engagement with difficult questions that may not ultimately have answers. In fact, a final answer may not even be the most propitious goal for an engaged and engaging archival theory.

Archivists face new, unprecedented challenges in many areas of their theories and work. Schwartz and Cook (2002) point out that the stakes are indeed, high, as the future of society's concepts of, needs for, and uses of the past are at risk. Archivists do not need to, indeed, should not, make these decisions on their own or in a vacuum. These decisions are critical to the continued vitality of the archive as a concept and as physical places. As archivists further consider the role subjective decision-making has in their theories and work, they would do well to avoid Derrida's (1991) archive fever that is described as: "to have a compulsive, repetitive, and nostalgic desire for the archive, an irrepressible desire to return to the origin, a homesickness, a nostalgia for the return to the most archaic place of absolute commencement" (p.91) in both their intellectual orientation as they consider new critiques and theories, and in their transformation of those theories into practice.

7. From Polders to Postmodernism

The history of archival theory has developed and changed, sometimes drastically, over the past 120 years. From the Dutch archivists who mirrored the consolidation of effort it took to create new land, or polders, from the North Sea in the Netherlands, to British and American archivists who clashed over the basic definitions of records, archives, and the role of the archivist, to more contemporary archivists who, from dispersed geographic locations, continue to ask questions within a postmodern framework that challenge nearly every aspect of archival theory, even the concept of the archive itself, archival theory has continued to develop in response to its many contexts. As such, archival paradigms have constantly shifted, as specific archival needs have required new theories and strategies to remain vital and viable.

The first century of professional archival theory has been rife with tension, debate, and most of all, change. The development of each archival paradigm was influenced by the preceding paradigm; each effort to change was, in part, initiated to resolve the tension between objectivity and subjectivity in the body of archival theory. The exception to this notion of resolution is the Questioning paradigm that seeks to exacerbate the tension in an effort to understand its composition. The tension between appraisal and custody, between passive and active archival practice, between history "as it happened" and communication through historical records is rooted in the discourse between subjectivity and objectivity in archival theory. The tension has never been fully resolved, however, since each new paradigm also assumed many of the concepts of its predecessors. Archival theory has accepted each paradigm change cumulatively rather than successively. Theorists today continue to discuss the importance and validity of the discrepancies between Jenkinson's and Schellenberg's theories.

After a thorough examination of each archival paradigm, a distinct periodicity begins to emerge. The first period of archival theory can be termed the Consolidation period. The Dutch Manual was written to give a specific and practical guide to Dutch archivists in regard to their dispersed collections. The Manual was written at a time when the Dutch government was focused on the centralization of archival collections and work. Through explicit and detailed instruction, the Dutch Manual focused on the arrangement and description of archival material that was, for the most part, medieval. These records were considered to be the most important documents retained from past Dutch government and religious entities. Muller, Feith, and Fruin define archives as collections of records that have been officially received or produced by an administrative body and were intended to remain in the custody of that body. The Dutch Manual describes archives as a living organism that changes with the function of its organization. The authors of the Manual were able to approach the concept of archival theory cautiously and sparingly, focus on practical considerations, and avoid an explicit discussion of appraisal altogether. The lack of explicit discussion of appraisal was due, in part, to the lack of need for appraisal in most archival holdings, but also because the authors of the Dutch Manual lacked a theoretical basis for such a discussion. The Dutch Manual was the first attempt at a cohesive and singular archival theory that would become the basis for much contemporary practice all over the world.

The role of the archivist in Muller, Feith, and Fruin's work can be described as records organizers. This role was somewhat ambiguous, as many archivists of the time were trained historians with interest and experience in diplomatics and paleography. The Dutch Manual reinforced this role through an emphasis on archival arrangement and description. The organization of records was an important point of emphasis in the Dutch Manual, which was used as a strategy to begin to condense archival practices into a single corpus of work.

The predominant users of the archives in the Consolidation period were historians in the mold of Ranke who sought to write history "as it happened." As such, these historians relied upon archives to provide consistent custody of records and to maintain the records of governments as they were created. Historians of the late 19th century relied heavily on the evidentiary uses of records in their work and considered the archive exclusively a repository of evidence.

In terms of appraisal and subjectivity, the Dutch Manual established a theoretical basis against individual archivists working in isolation with their own subjective, probably self-taught, guidelines. Though the text itself does not mention appraisal explicitly, Muller, Feith, and Fruin are extremely cautious in condoning individualized decision-making. It is important to recognize, however, that the Dutch Manual created a theoretical basis for appraisal through guidelines for best practices and its qualifications and definitions of archival records.Subjective decisions that are discussed in the Manual deal nearly exclusively with arrangement and description. Since the Dutch Manual is concerned with the consolidation and standardization of archival practice, one of its main purposes is to instill an objective orientation in its professional readers.

The second period of archival theory is the Reinforcement period. Jenkinson's focus is the reinforcement of the concepts in the Dutch Manual. Twenty-four years after the publication of the Dutch Manual, Sir Hilary Jenkinson published *A Manual of Archival Administration*. The Dutch Manual provided Jenkinson with a solid foundation upon which to build a new paradigm. This new paradigm was required because of Jenkinson's unique situation. Faced with varied types of records from temporary governmental organizations as a result of World War I, Jenkinson needed to create an archival theory that would allow for the creation of war archives, which would preserve the history of Britain's participation in the war within the broad archival context established by Muller, Feith, and Fruin. The Dutch Manual, with its detailed descriptions of arrangement specific to the Netherlands, was not entirely applicable to the situation. Jenkinson's work inherited a similar appreciation for accumulation, arrangement, and description as can be found in the Dutch Manual. Jenkinson reinforced the concepts in the Dutch Manual and expanded the professional responsibilities of the archivist as a result of the tensions between previous archival theory and new archival needs. He would argue, for the next 41 years, that archival theory should remain as objective as possible in order to retain the most accurate record of history possible.

Jenkinson devotes a significant portion of his Manual to the definition of archives, one of the points that distinguish his theory from the Dutch Manual. He defines archives as a substitute for memory; one that consists of records created and used during the course of an administration or organization's business. For Jenkinson, the definition of archives also includes their continued custody in archival institutions and the fact that records in archives are interrelated and dependent on context for meaning.

One of the most important contributions Jenkinson made to archival theory is his definition of the archivist as a professional. Jenkinson's role for the archivist is one of a keeper of records. In this role, the archivist was to focus on arrangement and description of archives, in a formal and professional manner. Direct service to the public was a secondary concern. Jenkinson was able to carve a niche for

CONCLUSION

archivists as distinct from both historians and librarians and created a clearly defined role for archivists to fulfill professionally. Like the Dutch Manual, Jenkinson's establishment of a professional status for archivists was based on objectivity in practice as well as theory. Unlike his Dutch predecessors, Jenkinson created a specific theoretical and professional niche for archivists to fill as the keeper of records.

The archivists who engaged in archival work during this time continued to primarily serve historians. The historians of the inter-war period were split into two distinct groups: the relativists such as Becker and Beard, who were active in the 1920s and early 1930s, and the more empirical historians working within the scientific historical paradigm. Both of these user groups relied on archives for evidence. The former group used archival holdings as material for interpretation and reinterpretation of history while the latter group of historians continued to rely upon archives for their narrative histories. It is during the Reinforcement period that archivists began to receive specialized training distinct from historians.

As professionals, Jenkinson encouraged archivists to not participate in appraisal decisions if at all possible. In the Reinforcement period, the archival paradigm was squarely focused on objectivity and the maintenance of truth in records. Jenkinson famously argued against appraisal as he understood the resulting destruction of records as a compromise of the integrity of the entire archive. If records were destroyed, it changed the meaning of all other related records.

The period immediately after World War II, much like the post-World War I professional crisis in England, produced a new set of challenges for archivists. This period in archival theory can be referred to as the Modern period. Theodore Schellenberg, who worked with the United States government and federal archives, was presented with an unprecedented increase in record bulk, rapidly changing technology, research interests that were dependent on access to records, and further unprecedented technological change in the form of expanded mechanical reproduction of records. The theoretical tools he had at his disposal in the form of the Dutch Manual and Jenkinson's Manual were unsuitable for the new types of archival tasks at hand.

Schellenberg's response to these issues was to develop a new archival paradigm that redefined records and archives. To that end, Schellenberg's focus was on the management of those records. His definition of the archive is, like Jenkinson's, based on the organic nature of archives. Schellenberg notes that archives are created in the course of activities undertaken to accomplish specific purposes. His definition is also pragmatic in that he includes the condition that archives be held in a manner that is safe from damage.

Schellenberg sought to reduce the number of records presented to the archivist for inclusion in the archive by allowing archivists the ability to make appraisal decisions. These decisions were to be made while archivists maintained the integrity and meaning of archived records in their original context. Allowing for appraisal decisions in his theory, Schellenberg promoted an increased level of subjectivity in shaping the archive. Schellenberg's role for the archivist can be termed records selectors.

Though they had theoretical disagreements, Schellenberg's paradigm, especially the role of the archivist, relies heavily and expands significantly upon the professional role introduced by Jenkinson. The professional recognition Jenkinson established for archivists as independent from historians is the basis from which Schellenberg's Modern paradigm would develop archivists' professional responsibilities. Schellenberg's expanded role for the archivist includes appraisal and subjective decisions, though not necessarily decisions guided exclusively by empirical principles.

CONCLUSION

The Modern archival paradigm focuses on what Schellenberg calls "records management," a theoretical approach which understands the archive to be the final destination for some, though not all, records produced by a given organization or government. Records management operates on the probable content of records based on the relative position of the record's creator rather than the specific content of the individual record. This higher-level approach to appraisal allows archivists to evaluate larger amounts of records very quickly without examining each record as well as limits record bulk in archives through destruction of unselected classes of records.

The records management approach to archives was a product of the need for an archival theory that matched the bureaucracy of the government in which it was created. Schellenberg worked in national government archives that were overloaded with records with only a further acceleration of bulk in view in the future. Historians and citizens also called for readily available records that stressed the need to reduce or eliminate the time between a record's time of inactivity and its availability in an archive. In the Modern paradigm, speed became a defining goal.

The users of Modern archives continued to be primarily professional historians, but were from different orientations in terms of writing history. Members of the Annales School and more empirical historians relied on archival sources for their innovative analyses. Social histories and political histories alike required evidence in the form of records. The former required higher levels of interpretation on the part of the historian, but the records that were the basis of these interpretations were assumed to be truthful and representative of action taken in the past.

While the Modern archival paradigm allowed for increased subjectivity for archivists to make their own appraisal decisions, it did so within a bureaucratic and increasingly empirical context. As historians were able to analyze historic data using computers, their practice steadily became more reliant upon statistical data in archival records. In contrast to aspects of British history at the turn of the 20th century, the focus of historical work became analysis rather than narrative. Schellenberg addressed these needs with a new archival paradigm that was controllable by large government entities, most importantly, the United States National Archives.

Schellenberg's embrace of appraisal as part of the Modern archival paradigm was a departure from past theories. While his own theories were focused on government archives that were implemented through bureaucratic means, Schellenberg's theory did allow for increased subjective decision-making on the part of archivists. The inclusion of the level of subjectivity in his theories helped establish Schellenberg as the founder of contemporary appraisal theory.

During the 1960s and 1970s, a cultural revolution took place in the United States and Western Europe. Various individuals, including African Americans, Native Americans, and women, just to name a few, began to demand equal treatment in the eyes of both culture and the law. Exemplified by the Civil Rights movement, these new demands would affect archivists directly. These demands included more open access to records and that records of previously underrepresented groups be kept along with more traditional types of records. This latest crisis in the archival profession was not a direct result of war, as the last two had been. Rather, the crisis that resulted in the Questioning archival paradigm was a cultural and social one, even larger in magnitude than the governmental changes in the Netherlands at the end of the 19th century.

In this new paradigm, archives were conceived as a means of communication. This followed the "literary turn"

CONCLUSION

in the study of history and historiography. The notion of the literary turn stated that the writing of history is a means of communication and, as such, could be read and criticized much like literary works. These shifts in orientation came from historiographers, cultural critics, and philosophers. Principles such as Truth and humanity's progressive journey toward perfection, that had enjoyed prominence since the Enlightenment, were questioned. The value of retaining records nearly exclusively of governments and dominant cultures was questioned in earnest.

In the Questioning paradigm, the definition of the archive reached its broadest aspect in the history of archival theory. Collections of records, regardless of their methods of accumulation, were considered archives. The archivists who created the Questioning paradigm actively sought out records to add to archival collections and took an active role in the archiving of governments and organizations as well as other, less traditional sources of records. Rather than a simple accumulation of material, the archive itself was assumed to be an expression of the archivist's point of view.

The role for the archivist in this contemporary paradigm is that of records questioner. Not satisfied to take traditional archival theory at face value, these archivists asked questions of the hierarchies of power in the archive and sought to understand its history and implementation over time. In fact, these five archivists, Brothman, Cook, Heald, Ketelaar, and MacNeil are the first to conceive of their paradigm in archival theory as such. The role of the archivist is defined as active and as a professional who changes his or her own work from "archives" to "archiving" (Cook, 2000). Self-consciously, these archivists have developed new appraisal theories, such as Cook's Macroappraisal, that attempt to encompass more users' perspectives in terms of government interaction.

Another result of this type of questioning is the notion of the post-custodial archives. First established by Gerald Ham (1975 and 1981), a post-custodial approach to archives that includes an emphasis "away from a concentration on storage of a relatively small volume of information-rich paper archives towards the management of archives in a variety of formats, irregularly created, of unpredictable value as sources of information, and above all existing in massive volume," (Flynn, 2001). The post-custodial approach to archival information emphasizes the notion that contemporary archivists can no longer be expected to be a keeper of records, passive or otherwise. Through changing the definition of the archival record and defining a new role for the archivist, a post-custodial approach to the records continuum acts on the questions asked by archivists working within the Questioning paradigm.

Further influences on the Questioning paradigm include historians who wrote new social histories of underrepresented peoples and who gleaned information from archival sources but mostly from negative space. These historians found information about their areas of interest by what was not written or retained. Identity politics solidified in the academy and began to question the validity of an institution that had not responded quickly to the needs of its users. Philosophers and critics began to ask specific questions regarding archives and the creation of social and cultural memory.

The five archivists who responded to these philosophers and critics began to reframe archival theory in a new, postmodern context. These archivists took subjective decision-making as valid in its attempts to define the archive through appraisal. The theorists in the Questioning paradigm encouraged archivists to include self-reflexive questions in their primarily practice-oriented work. Appraisal, and its subjective decisions, was viewed as an obvious aspect of archival work. With issues of bulk to consider, the Questioning paradigm encouraged archivists to implement appraisal based on their own decisions and criteria.

This paradigm is the most recent cohesive archival paradigm to have been created. Since intellectual history tends to shift significantly with every new generation, another paradigm shift is probably on the horizon within the next ten to twenty years. Will the shift be toward more networked, computer-based archiving or will the new paradigm be in reaction to the increased subjective responsibility given to archivists over the past 50 years? Most likely, the shift will be born out of a crisis in some regard, perhaps a crisis in the retention and accessibility of digital records?

As archives themselves are products of an entity, organization, or government, archivists are professionally placed between the demands of the entity they serve and their own professional theories and practices. As illustrated above, archival theory and practice are created within the contexts of cultures and societies. The values in each culture inform the archive through valuation of different types and sets of information. These values are passed on to the archivist both implicitly and explicitly. From the research presented here, four key factors that have, over the past 120 years, affected the creation, content, and focus of each archival paradigm to emerge. These factors are geography, history, historiography, and technological change.

Each of the paradigms discussed above come from countries with specific and independent archival needs created as a function of varied geographic location. Especially before the relatively recent introduction of international professional development in archives, the geographic factor played a very important role by isolating archivists in their own theoretical situations.

During the end of the 19th century, the Dutch were concerned with the consolidation of their national archival holdings as they developed a new government from smaller local governments. This consolidation required that archivists have a robust theory with clear directives to work toward in their archives. Jenkinson's England, while traditionally separate from the rest of continental Europe, was faced with a unique set of issues after World War I. Since most of the war had been fought away from the British Isles, archival facilities were intact, for the most part, and ready to receive archives from the war. England's historically liberal and enlightened government contributed to the need for an archival theory distinct from both European and North American traditions as their government remained unique among both democracies and monarchies of the time. It is well documented that Schellenberg intentionally created a new approach to archives in order to better work with high volumes of records. By virtue of his work in the United States, it is clear that the unique governmental and cultural aspects of the United States contributed to the development of a unique approach to archives. Also, the United States enjoyed a relatively new set of archives to work with, for example, archives with no medieval records, which is perhaps why Schellenberg was able to create a paradigm that focused on how records were brought into the archive. The Questioning paradigm is a more international paradigm, but its origins are firmly in the North American/Western European tradition. Also, it can be argued that this paradigm has been created in a post-nationalist context, one in which national boundaries are crossed more easily and a professional emphasis on collaboration exists, thereby changing the impact of the geographic factor without eliminating it.

Since the archivists who wrote much of the theory discussed above were involved with government archives, it is logical that their paradigms would match needs of specific governmental and national situations. It is surprising, then,

CONCLUSION

that each of these new paradigms were assimilated into the canon of archival theory since the context of each paradigm's creation is highly specific. The assimilation of new theoretical paradigms was completed, however, at an even deeper level than that of archival practice. Levels of interpretation occur between archival theory and its implementation as practice. The act of interpretation, in this case, contributes to subjectivity in archival practice. As such, it is important to note since this interpretation allows archivists in various geographic locations the opportunity to adapt archival theory for their own uses.

The second factor which influences archival theory is the immediate past history of the period in which the theory was developed. Archivists and historians work closely together, and influence one another through their theories and practices. Archives have long been the repositories of primary sources used by historians for their work. This factor has less to do with the history being written from archival sources and more with the immediate influence of events that occur at the time the archival paradigm is created.

Each paradigm has its own examples to illustrate this point. For the Dutch, the history written during the end of the 19th century was highly empirical and followed Ranke's maxim of writing history "as it happened." Dutch archival theory followed this trend, especially since so many archivists of the time were trained historians. Perhaps the most obvious example of the influence of contemporary history in the development of archival theory is the Modern paradigm. Between Jenkinson's Reinforcement and Schellenberg's Modern paradigms, the writing of history took a severe turn toward the subjective. Lead by American historians Becker and Beard, the subjective movement in the writing of history followed the increasingly popular notion that individual interpretation was the root of more history than empirical objectivity (Novick, 1988). Eventually, subjectivity in values would be blamed for the rise of fascism in Europe, which lead to the Holocaust and World War II (Wolin, 2004). As a result, historians and cultures around the world turned toward objectivity as a scientific mechanism of balance to keep subjective and despotic powers in check.

It is within this contemporary history that Schellenberg created the Modern archival paradigm. Archivists at the time worked with records that ranged from the first saved records to the most recent to enter the archive. Historians wrote histories of various time periods, from ancient to contemporary. Each group was influenced by not only the previous professional paradigms in which they participated, but also within the historical context of their time. This is how Schellenberg's work can allow for more subjective appraisal while still adhering to notions of theoretical objective empiricism.

The Questioning paradigm derives its motivation, in part, from the study of identity politics and diversity, both of which came to the forefront of academic study in the 1980s and 1990s. In fact, many of the questions that are asked of the archive within the Questioning paradigm are about diversity and representation in the archive. For both identity politics and diversity, equal representation is very important, as it is one locus of power in the continued struggle for recognition in all aspects of life, including evidence of action taken by governments and organizations.

The third factor that has influenced every archival paradigm is the historiographical factor. This factor is closely linked to the second context as the writing of history is to the study of the writing of history. What is unique about this context, however, is timing. Archivists, by the nature of the profession, have to react to cultural expectations rather than being proactive. This is especially the case

CONCLUSION

in the earlier archival paradigms where archivists were encouraged not to change their practice or theories based on contemporary views of historical material.

Regardless, even the advocates for a "timeless" archive must, in some capacity, react to the contemporary analysis of the writing of history in the form of historiography. For the Dutch, this meant following those who accepted Ranke's objective historical practice. The Dutch Manual is concerned with the replication of specific arrangement and description strategies in order to standardize access to primary historical sources. As illustrated above in the Reinforcement paradigm, Jenkinson work was published between changes that happened in the study of history and the context of historiography. The two paradigms shifted at different rates: as the historical paradigm shifted toward Becker and Beard's subjectivity, the historiographical paradigm remained oriented toward objectivity. Since historiography must necessarily follow the writing of history, this paradigm will always be second to change. Archival paradigms are third to change since historiographical analysis is the final step in the evaluation and periodization of the writing of history. In this case, Jenkinson's strict adherence to objectivity was counter to the historical context, but in line with the historiographical context. When Schellenberg created the Modern paradigm, the historiographical context had returned to a strict objectivity in the wake of fascist despotism. For the Questioning paradigm, historiography was highly influential in terms of establishing the paradigm itself. These archivists focused on history as interpretation, thereby creating an interpretive role for the professional archivist as well. The historiographical factor is complex and can create a whip-like effect on archival theory due to changes of historical opinion over time and the necessary lag in changes as a result of changes in historiography.

The further effect of the historiographical context is that the archivists who create a new archival paradigm do not necessarily see its apogee during their professional lives. As the evolution of a paradigm proceeds, newly trained archivists become practitioners and theorists in their own right, and supplant the originators of a paradigm. Through interpretation and practice, paradigms change until, eventually, a professional crisis occurs and a new paradigm is created in place of the old. This is another way in which archival paradigms are necessarily a few steps behind the vanguard of cultural change, even within the profession.

The fourth, and perhaps most important to all contemporary archivists, factor to affect archival theory is the technological factor. Technological change has been the impetus for nearly every archival paradigm shift. The usual results of technological change are increased numbers of records, which create a need for new theoretical approaches and modifications to practice.

The Consolidation paradigm was, in contrast to every other paradigm, only indirectly affected by technological change. While one could argue that the technological change in the industrial revolution in Europe affected the Netherlands in a negative way, the direct impact is relegated to means of transportation and communication. Changes in these areas allowed local archives to contribute material over long distances in a shorter amount of time.

It is with the Reinforcement paradigm that the technological factor begins to have a real impact on the development of archival theory. Jenkinson experienced the rapid development of technology for warfare and communication. While the telephone and typewriter were relatively new technologies at the time, their impact was recorded in Jenkinson's theories, though mostly in a disparaging manner. The telephone decreased the number of printed records available to archive, while the typewriter changed how administrators viewed the creation of the record. According to Jenkinson, the typewriter allowed records creators to create records first and think about their utility later. This attitude, combined with exponential increases in other technological capabilities, would be the impetus for the next archival paradigm change.

The Modern paradigm was created in direct response to technological changes that created an unprecedented number of records presented to government archives in the United States. Communications technology, bolstered by their necessary development during World War II, expanded into different areas that included the mechanical reproduction of paper documents. Schellenberg developed an archival theory that addressed these issues and allowed only records deemed valuable enough in terms of information or as artifacts in the archive.

The Questioning paradigm has also been shaped by the technological factor. This factor has had increasing influence on archival theory during the last half of the 20th century. Archivists are now working with various digital formats that could not have been conceived of even 20 years ago, much less 100. As with other technological changes, the number of records made available to archive has increased. With computing power increasing exponentially, archivists will increasingly feel the implications of the technological context in both the creation and the practice of their theories.

An example of the impact of the technological factor is the proposition of reconsidering Jenkinson's idea of disallowing appraisal activities in the archive (Duranti & MacNeil, 1996). The basic notion is that if electronic records can be searched by keywords along with other sources of information, and electronic storage continues to be readily and relatively cheaply available, why not save everything? It is this type of thinking that prompted Gerald Ham to establish the notion of post-custodial archives. Archivists who work with digital datasets and records that do not necessarily contain constant data have little choice but to acquiesce to the notion that they are not the keepers of many electronic records. With different limits of physical space, the imperative to appraise digital records is lower than with paper records. As records creators and archivists alike become more reliant on digital technology, electronic records and post-custodial issues will continue to increase in importance in terms of both practice and theory.

Considerations of technological and economic limits will play a large role in the creation of the next archival paradigm, regardless of timing. As archivists increasingly interact with and rely on computers to not only hold and access catalogs and union lists, but to access records themselves, the technological context will become even more important than it is today.

In order for the archival profession to continue on its trajectory of increasing professionalization, it is important to recognize the differences and similarities in archival paradigms. While archivists should indeed subscribe to a panoply of archival theories, it is important to the profession that they also engage in a self-conscious discourse on their work. One way to accomplish this is to continue to view the archival profession as emerging into its own distinct and malleable profession.

Over the past 110 years, archival theory has undergone significant changes. This has led, in part, to the definition of the archival profession as an independent, separate from historical research and the writing of history. This text has argued that an investigation into the development of archival paradigms and the importance of the intellectual history of archival theory is itself an indication that the archival profession continues to develop its own unique and independent professional history and context.

CONCLUSION

While there are no definitive answers to the questions posed by the changes in archival paradigms, the continued study of change in archival theory is important to the vitality and understanding of the profession. If archives continue to receive a cultural as well as legal mandate for the information they contain, understanding theoretical paradigms will become even more important than in the past. Continuing to engage and develop a discourse within archival theory will allow for a robust understanding of the development of the archival profession over time.

References

"Annales school" Dictionary of the Social Sciences. Craig Calhoun, ed. Oxford University Press 2002. Oxford Reference Online. Oxford University Press. UC - Berkeley Library. 4 April 2008 <http://www.oxfordreference.com/views/ENTRY.html?subview=Main&entry=t104.e63>

Appleby, J., Hunt, L., & Jacob, M. (1994). *Telling the truth about history*. New York: W. W. Norton and Company.

Bantin, P. C. (1998). Strategies for managing electronic records: A new archival paradigm? An affirmation of our archival traditions? *Archival Issues, 23*(1), 17-34.

Barritt, M. R. (2003). Coming to America: Dutch archivistiek and American archival practice. In *Manual for the arrangement and description of archives* (pp. xxxiv-l). Chicago: The Society of American Archivists.
(Reprinted from *Archival Issues,* 1993, 18, pp. 43-54).

van Bath, B. S. (1948). Guide to the work of Dutch Mediaevalists, 1919-1947. *Speculum, 23*, 236-266. Retrieved May 8, 2006, from JSTOR database: http://links.jstor.org/sici?sici=0038-7134%28194804%2923%3A2%3C236%3AGTTWOD%3E2.0.CO%3B2-O

Baudrillard, J. O. (1981). *Simulacra and simulation* (S. F. Glaser, Trans.). Ann Arbor, MI: University of Michigan.

Bearman, D. (1989). *Archival methods* (Rep. No. 9). Pittsburgh: Archives and Museum Informatics. Retrieved March 30, 2007, from http://www.archimuse.com/publishing/archival_methods/index.html

Bearman, D. (1994). Archival strategies. *American Archivist, 58*, 374-407. Retrieved March 30, 2007, from http://www.archimuse.com/publishing/archival_strategies/index.html

Boles, F., & Young, J. M. (1985). Exploring the black box: The appraisal of
university administrative records. *American Archivist, 48(2),* 121-140.

Booms, H. (1987). Society and the formation of a documentary heritage: Issues in the appraisal of archival sources. *Archivaria, 24*, 69-107. Edited and Translated by Hermin Joldersma and Richard Klumpenhouwer.

Brothman, B. (1991). Orders of value: Probing the theoretical terms of archival practice, *Archivaria 32,* 78-100.

Brown, R. (1992). Records acquisition strategy and its theoretical foundation: The case for a concept of archival hermeneutics. *Archivaria, 33*, 34-56.

Bulkley, M. E. (1922). *Bibliographical survey of contemporary sources for the economic and social history of the war.* Oxford: The Clarendon Press.

Cannon, J. (Ed.). (1997). Record offices. In *Oxford companion to British history* (p. 792). New York: Oxford University Press.

Chafe, W. H., & Sitkoff, H. (Eds.). (1991). *A history of our time: Readings on postwar America*. New York: Oxford University Press.

Contemporary Authors Online, Gale, 2006. Reproduced in *Biography Resource Center*. Farmington Hills, Mich.: Thomson Gale. 2006. http://galenet.galegroup.com.ezproxy.sfpl.org/servlet/BioRC

Cook, T. (1997). What's past is prologue: A history of archival ideas since 1898, and the future paradigm shift. *Archivaria 43*. Retrieved on March 27, 2007 from: http://www.mybestdocs.com/cookt-pastprologue-ar43fnl.htm

Cook, T. (1999, April 21). *Archival appraisal and collection: Issues, challenges, new approaches*. Lecture presented at the Special Lecture Series to the University of Maryland and NARA Staff, College Park, MD.

Cook, T. (2000). Archival science and postmodernism: New formulations for old concepts. *Archival Science 1*, 3-24.

Cook, T. (2001). Fashionable nonsense or professional rebirth: Postmodernism and the practice of archives. *Archivaria 51*, 14-35.

Cook, T. and J. M. Schwartz (2002). Archives, records, and power: From (postmodern) theory to (archival) performance. *Archival Science 2*, pp. 171-185.

Derrida, J. (1995). *Archive fever: A Freudian impression* (E. Prenowitz, Trans.). Chicago: University of Chicago Press.

Duranti, L. (1994). The concept of appraisal and archival theory. *American Archivist, 57*(2), 328-344.

Duranti, L., & MacNeil, H. (1996). The protection of the integrity of electronic records: An overview of the UBC-MAS research project. *Archivaria, 42,* 64.

Eastwood, T. E. (2002). Introduction to 2003 reissue. In R. H. Ellis & P. Walne (Eds.), *Selected writings of Sir Hilary Jenkinson* (pp. vii-xx) [Introduction]. Chicago: The Society of American Archivists.

Ellis, R. H., & Walne, P. (2003). Editors' preface. In R. H. Ellis & P. Walne (Eds.), *Selected writings of Sir Hilary Jenkinson* (pp. 11-12) [Preface]. Chicago: The Society of American Archivists.

Faculty biographical information. (2007, March 12). School of Library, Archival, and Information Studies. Retrieved March 30, 2007, from University of British Columbia Web site:
http://www.slais.ubc.ca/PEOPLE/faculty/faculty-bio/macneil-bio.htm

Flynn, S.J. A. (2001). The records continuum model in context and its implications for archival practice. *Journal of the Society of Archivists, 22:1,* 79-93.

Foucault, M. (1970). *The order of things: An archaeology of the human sciences.* (A.M. Sheridan Smith, Trans.) New York: Random House.

Foucault, M. (1972). *The archaeology of knowledge.* (A.M. Sheridan Smith, Trans.) New York: Pantheon Books.

Fredriksson, B. (2003). Postmodernistic archival science: Rethinking the methodology of a science. *Archival Science, 3,* 177-197.

Fukuyama, F. (1992). *The end of history and the last man.* New York: Free Press.

Greene, M., & Daniels-Howell, T. (1997). Documentation with an attitude: A pragmatist's guide to the selection and acquisition of business records. In J. M. O'Toole (Ed.), *The records of American business* (pp. 161-206). Chicago: Society of American Archivists.

Ham, F. G. (1975). The archival edge. *American Archivist, 38,* 5-13.

Ham, F. G. (1981). Archival strategies for the post-custodial era. *American Archivist, 44,* 207-216.

Hamilton, C., Harris, V. and Reid, G. (Eds.) (2002). *Refiguring the archive.* Norwell, MA: Kluwer Academic.

Harris, V. (1997). Claiming less, delivering more: A critique of positivist formulations on Archives in South Africa. *Archivaria, 44,* 132-141.

Harris, V. (2004, April). *The cultured archive: An interrogation of the nexus between archive and culture from a South African perspective.* Keynote speech presented at the conference Archives in Multicultural Societies, Oslo, Norway.

Heald, C. (1996). Is there room for archives in the postmodern world? *American Archivist, 59,* 88-101.

Horsman, P., Ketelaar, E., & Thomassen, T. (2003). Introduction to the 2003 reissue. In A. H. Leavitt (Trans.), *Manual for the arrangement and description of archives* (Reissue ed., pp. v-xxxiii) [Introduction]. Chicago: The Society of American Archivists. (Original work published 1898).

The second international conference on the history of records and archives (ICHORA-2) (2005). Retrieved September 11, 2006, from
http://i-chora2.archiefschool.nl/speakers.php

Jenkinson, H. (1922). *A manual of archive administration*. Economic and social history of the World War (British series). Oxford: The Clarendon Press.

Jenkinson, H. (2003). Modern archives: Some reflections on T. R. Schellenberg. In R. H. Ellis & P. Walne (Eds.), *Selected writings of Sir Hilary Jenkinson* (pp. 339-343). Chicago: The Society of American Archivists. (Reprinted from *Journal of the Society of Archivists*, 1956, *I*, pp. 147-149).

Jones, H. G. (2002). Introduction to the 2003 reissue. In *Modern archives: Principles and techniques* (pp. xi-xii) [Introduction]. Chicago: Society of American Archivists. (Original work published 1956).

Kaplan, E. (2002). Many paths to partial truths: Archives, anthropology, and the power of representation. *Archival Science, 2*, 209-220.

Ketelaar, E. (2006) *C.V.* Retrieved September 13, 2006 from:
http://cf.hum.uva.nl/bai/home/eketelaar/cve.html

Ketelaar, E. (2004). Time future contained in time past: Archival science in the 21st century. *Journal of the Japan Society for Archival Science, 1*, 20-35. Retrieved May 11, 2006, from http://cf.hum.uva.nl/bai/home/eketelaar/publication.html

Ketelaar, E. (2002). Archival temples, archival prisons: Modes of power and protection. *Archival Science 2*, 221-238.

Ketelaar, E. (2001). Tacit narratives: The meanings of archives. *Archival Science I*, 131-141.

Kuhn, T. S. (1996). *The structure of scientific revolutions* (3rd ed.). Chicago: University of Chicago. (Original work published 1962)

Leavitt, A. H. (2003). Translator's preface. In A. H. Leavitt (Trans.), *Manual for the arrangement and description of archives* (2nd ed., pp. 7-8) [Preface]. Chicago: The Society of American Archivists. (Original work published 1898).

Leventhal, F. (Ed.). (1995). History. In *Twentieth-century Britain: An encyclopedia* (pp. 362-363). New York: Garland.

Loewen, C. (1992). From human neglect to planetary survival: New approaches to the appraisal of environmental records. *Archivaria, 33*, 87-103.

Lyotard, J-F (1984). *The postmodern condition: A report on knowledge.* (Trans. Geoffrey Bennington and Brian Massumi). Minneapolis: University of Minnesota Press. (Original work published in 1979).

MacNeil, H. (1994). Archival theory and practice: Between two paradigms. *Archivaria, 37*, 6-20.

McKemmish, S. (2001). Evidence of me .... *Archives and Manuscripts, 29*(1). Retrieved March 28, 2006, from http://www.mybestdoc.com/mckemmish-s-evidofme-ch10.htm

Menne-Haritz, A. (1994). Appraisal or documentation: Can we appraise archives by selecting content? *American Archivist, 57*(3), 528-542.

Moore, L. J. (2008). *Restoring order: The Ecole des Chartes and the development of libraries and archives in France, 1820-1870.* Duluth, Minnesota: Litwin Books.

Morton, D. (2000). *Off the record: The technology and culture of sound recording in America.* Camden: The Rutgers University Press.

Muller, S. Feith, J.A., and Fruin, R. (2003). *Manual for the arrangement and description of archives.* (Trans. Arthur H. Leavitt). Chicago: The Society of American Archivists. (Original work published in 1898).

New Deal. (2008). In *Encyclopædia Britannica.* Retrieved May 6, 2008, from Encyclopædia Britannica Online: http://search.eb.com/eb/article-9055453

Norton, M. C. (1940). Manual for the description of archives [review article]. *The Mississippi Valley Historical Review, 27*, 319-320. Retrieved May 11, 2006, from JSTOR database.

Novick, P. (1988). *That noble dream: The "objectivity question" and the American historical profession*. Cambridge: Cambridge University Press.

Norris, C. (2005). "Linguistic turn," In *The Oxford Companion to Philosophy*. Oxford University Press. Oxford Reference Online. Oxford University Press. UC - Berkeley Library. Retrieved June 1, 2008 from: http://www.oxfordreference.com/views/ENTRY.html?subview=Main&entry=t116.e1434

Popper, K. (2002). *Conjectures and refutations: The growth of scientific knowledge*. New York: Routledge. (Original work published 1963).

Ribeiro, F. (2001). Archival science and changes in the paradigm. *Archival Science 1*, 295-310.

Rumschottel, H. (2001). The development of archival science as a scholarly discipline. *Archival Science, 1*, 143-155.

Samuels, H. (1992). Improving our disposition: Documentation strategy. *Archivaria, 33*, 125-140.

Schellenberg, T. R. (2003). *Modern archives: Principles and techniques*. Chicago: Society of American Archivists. (Original work published 1956).

Schwartz, J. M. and Cook, T. (2002). "Archives, records, and power: The making of modern memory. *Archival Science 2*, 1-19.

Shepherd, E. (1997). The American school. In *Theories of appraisal*. Retrieved August 1, 2006, from University

College, London, School of Library, Archive, and Information Science Web site:
http://www.ucl.ac.uk/~uczcw09/appraisl/level1.htm

Social history. *A Dictionary of Sociology*. John Scott and Gordon Marshall. Oxford University Press 2005. Oxford Reference Online. Oxford University Press. UC - Berkeley Library. Retrieved June 1, 2008 from: http://www.oxfordreference.com/views/ENTRY.html?subview=Main&entry=t88.e2139

Swoyer, C. (Spring 2003 Edition). Relativism. *The Stanford encyclopedia of philosophy*, Edward N. Zalta (ed.). Retrieved March 22, 2007, from: http://plato.stanford.edu/archives/spr2003/entries/relativism/

Tilly, L and Scott, J. W. (1978). *Women, work and family.* New York: Holt, Rinehart and Winston.

Tschan, R. (2002). A comparison of Jenkinson and Schellenberg on appraisal. T*he American Archivist, 65*, 176-195.

Upward, F. (1998). *In search of the continuum: Ian Maclean's 'Australian experience' essays on recordkeeping.* Caulfield, Victoria, Australia: Monash University, Continuum Research Group. Retrieved May 13, 2006, from http://www.sims.monash.edu.au/research/rcrg/publications/fuptrc.html

Upward, Frank and McKemmish, S. (Eds.) Institutionalizing the Archival Document" in *Archival Documents*, eds. Sue McKemmish and Frank Upward (Melbourne, Ancora Press, 1993),41-54.

White, H. L. (2003). Modern archives: Principles and techniques (pp. xv-xvi) [Foreword]. Chicago: Society of American Archivists. (Original work published 1956).

White, H. V. (1975). *Metahistory: The historical imagination in 19th century Europe.* Baltimore: Johns Hopkins University Press.

Wolin, R. (2004). *The seduction of unreason: The intellectual romance with fascism from Nietzsche to postmodernism.* Princeton, NJ: Princeton University Press.

Index

A
American Archivist 114
American dream 72
American exceptionalism 73
American Historical Association 76
Andrews, C. M. 80
Ankersmit, F. R. 109
Antiwar movement 107
Appraisal theory
  controversies over 3, 66, 143
  factors contributing to 4, 63, 99
  See also Dutch Manual; Manual of Archive Administration, A; Modern Archives: Principles and Techniques; Questioning Paradigm
Archival Appraisal of Records Containing Personal Information: A RAMP Study With Guidelines 116
Archival theory
  consolidation of 21-52, 143
  contexts in creation of 7-19, 69-70, 153-155
  critical theory 1-2
  efficiency 75
  objectivity 19, 29, 75, 91, 143, 157
  periods of 144-150
  study of 1
  subjectivity 4-5, 19, 29, 34-35, 88, 90, 118, 143, 157
  technology 1, 160
  See also Dutch Manual, Manual of Archive Administration, A, Modern Archives: Principles and Techniques, Questioning Paradigm
Archivaria 114-116
Archive Fever 105, 140-141
Archives
  and art 1
  citizens' expectations of 72, 111
  cooperation between 50-51
  duplication of records 12-13, 43, 86, 159
  post-custodial 152
  war archives 48-51, 67, 146
  See also United Kingdom
  See also Canada, Netherlands, United King-

dom, United States for archives in those countries
See also Definitions of archives
Archivists' professionalism *See* Professionalism
Archivists' roles *See* Role of the archivist
Authenticity 12, 14, 58

B

Bacon, Francis 25
Baudriallard, Jean 121
Bauer, Philip 75
Beard, Charles 63-65, 147, 155
Becker, Carl 63-65, 147, 155
Benjamin, Walter 64
Boorstin, Daniel J. 73
British Economic and Social History of the World Series (book series) 59
Brooks, Philip C. 89
Brothman, Brien 101, 113
See also Questioning paradigm
Butler, Judith 122

C

Canada
archives 112-114, 116, 154
Canadian Historical Association *Journal* 116
Canadian Library Journal 114

Civil Rights movement 107, 150
Civilian Conservation Corps 71
Computers in archives 12-14, 159-160
See also Technology
Conflict between Jenkinson and Schellenberg's theories 69-70, 76, 78, 81-83, 86-89, 91-92
See also Jenkinson, Sir Hilary, Schellenberg, Theodore Roosevelt
Consolidation paradigm *See* Dutch Manual
Contemporary archival paradigm
See Questioning paradigm
Cook, Terry 101, 116, 129
See also Macroappraisal, Questioning paradigm
Custody 41

D

Definitions of archives 1, 31-32, 47, 50, 80-82, 111, 143
See also Dutch Manual, Manual of Archive Administration, A, Modern Archives: Principles and

INDEX

Techniques, Questioning Paradigm
Definitions of records 32, 41-42, 49, 53-54, 78-79, 81-83
  See also Dutch Manual, Manual of Archive Administration, A, Modern Archives: Principles and Techniques, Questioning Paradigm
Derrida, Jacques 127, 134, 136-137
  See also Archive Fever
Descartes, Rene 25
Diplomatics 79
Documents *See* Records
Dutch Manual 21-52
  appraisal 31, 144-145
  arrangement 32-35, 40, 144-145
  provenance 33-34, 37
  provenienzprinzip 33
  r*egistraturprinzip* 33
  concepts 21, 32-33, 49
  consolidation of theory 22-26, 36-40
  contemporary interpretations of 28, 38-39
  context of writing 21-25, 144
  criticism of 38-39, 60-63
  definition of archives 31-32, 35, 144
  definition of records 32
  description 32, 35-36, 145
  objectivity 32, 36, 40, 145
  role of the archivist 24, 42, 47, 52, 144
  standardization of archival theory 23-24, 29,
  subjectivity 32, 34, 38, 40, 145
  tension 29-30, 36, 40
  theory 28, 30-32, 36-39, 144-145

E

Electronic records 104, 153, 159-160
  See also Technology
Electronic Records Practice: Lessons from the National Archives of Canada 116
England *See* United Kingdom
England Under Queen Anne 46
Epistemology 28, 36-38, 66, 81, 94, 98, 101, 123

F

Feith, Johan A. 21, 27
  See also Dutch Manual
Foucualt, Michel 126-127
Fruin, Robert 21, 27
  See also Dutch Manual

G

Genius of American Politics, The 73
Genovese, Elizabeth Fox 109
Great Britain *See* United Kingdom
Great Depression, The 63, 72, 79

H

Ham, Gerald 152, 159
Handleiding voor het Ordenen en Beschrijven van Archieven See Dutch Manual
Heald, Carolyn 101, 114
  See also Questioning paradigm
Historians
  and scientific history 25-26, 46, 84
  Annales School 18, 149
  approach to their work 25, 44-47, 98
  professional links to archivists 2, 26, 39-40, 45, 74, 85, 95, 98, 147, 155
  See also Study of history, The
Historiography 7-8, 109-110, 157
  influence on archival theory 14-19, 63-64, 72-73, 105, 109, 155-157
  linguistic turn 108-109, 117, 119, 123
  See also Study of history, The
History *See* Study of history, The
Hume, David 45

I

Imagining Archives: Essays and Reflections by Hugh A. Taylor 116
International Council on Archives 48, 115-116
Institute on the Preservation and Administration of Archives 85

J

Jenkinson, Sir Hilary 40-68, 119
  biography 47-49
  comparison to Schellenberg's theories *See* Conflict between Jenkinson and Schellenberg's theories
  professional history 47-49
  See also Manual of Archive Administration, A

K

Kahn, Herman 75
Ketelaar, Eric 101, 115

See also Questioning paradigm
Kuhn, Thomas 9
See also Paradigm shifts

L

Lesy, Michael 109
Librarians 78, 85, 147
Literary turn 151
Lord Grey of the Reform Bill 46

M

MacNeil, Heather 101, 115
See also Questioning paradigm
Maitland, Frederick 46
Man in the Gray Flannel Suit, The 73
Manual for the Arrangement and Description of Archives
See Dutch Manual
Manual of Archive Administration, A 41-68
　accumulation of records 54
　　appraisal 54-55, 60-61, 66, 147, 159-160
　archival arrangement 47, 50, 60-61, 146
　　fonds 60-61
　　provenance 53
　authenticity 58
　　concepts 47, 56-58, 61-62, 97-99
　consolidation of theory 47
　contemporary interpretations of 64
　context of writing 42-48, 63-64, 68
　criticism of 63-67
　custody 41, 58, 146
　definition of archives 47, 49, 51-53, 65, 81, 146
　definition of records 41-42, 49, 53-54
　evidentiary uses of records 54-55, 58
　objectivity 42, 47, 56, 60, 67, 146-147
　original order 54, 68
　records creators 50, 54
　reinforcement of previous theories 49-63, 66, 68, 146
　role of the archivist 42, 47, 52, 55-57, 61-63, 65, 68, 146-147
　subjectivity 42, 58-63, 67
　tension 66
　theory 41, 51, 62
　truth 58-59, 67
　See also Jenkinson, Sir Hilary
McCarthy, Joseph 74
Metahistory 108
Macroappraisal 129, 152
　See also Cook, Terry

Modern Archives: Principles and Techniques 69-99
  appraisal 70, 77-81, 83-84, 85-88, 148-150
  concepts 77-78, 93, 98
  consolidation of archives 74
  context of writing 70-71, 77, 91, 156
  criticism of 96-97, 99
  decentralization 86-87, 93
  definition of archives 80-82, 88, 148
  definition of records 78-79, 81-84, 86, 94
  disposition plans 94
  efficiency 69-70, 81-83, 92-93, 98
  evidentiary uses of records 87, 95
  fonds 78, 87
  governmental influence 80-81
  objectivity 91
  pragmatism 69, 81
  records bulk 70-72, 78-79, 90, 92, 97, 148
  records creators 86-87, 90, 95
  records management 69, 78, 85-86, 90, 93-94, 97, 148-149
  role of the archivist 74-75, 79, 85-90, 95, 97, 148-149
  standardization of archival theory 74, 93-94
  subjectivity 83-84, 88, 90-95, 148, 150
  theory 69, 77-78, 80
  truth 79, 90, 97-98
  value of records 87-88, 90
  See also Schellenberg, Theodore Roosevelt
Modern paradigm *See Modern Archives: Principles and Techniques*
Muller, Samuel 21, 27-28
  See also Dutch Manual

N
Netherlands
  archival theory 10, 22-25, 39-40, 51, 154-155
  archives 23-24, 45, 112, 115-116, 144, 146
  early archives 10-11, 47
  Royal Society of Dutch Archivists 116

O
Oegg, Josef Anton 22

P
Paradigm shifts 7-10, 61, 63, 87, 111-112, 158
  See also Kuhn, Thomas
Popper, Karl 10
Professionalism 2, 19, 48, 57, 69, 79, 146-147
Provenance *See Respect des fonds*

Q

Questioning paradigm 101-141
  administrative aspects 119
  appraisal 111, 124, 129, 135-136, 139-140, 152-153
  archives 101, 111, 117, 140
  communication 117, 122, 151
  context 102-103, 126, 135-136, 156
  critical theory 101-102, 105-106, 126-127, 139, 151
  cultural aspects 119-120, 130-131, 133, 150, 156
  definition of records 110-111, 124-127
  definition of the archive 151
  diversity 106, 113, 151, 156
  fonds 117, 121, 135
  electronic records 104, 110, 119
  historical orientation 101, 121-122, 127-128, 131
  historiography 105, 108-109
  identity 130
  inherited practice 127-128
  interpretation 101, 117-118, 122, 124-125, 134, 139, 155
  memory 106, 111, 126, 135
  metanarrative 105, 117
  narrative 131, 136
  objectivity 118, 121-122, 132-139
  paradigm change 102, 111-112, 118, 151
  poetics 119
  postmodern critical theory 104-105, 108, 114, 117-118, 120-124, 139-140, 152
  power 125, 127, 130, 134, 137-138
  records creators 134
  role of the archivist 103, 119, 121, 125, 130-132, 151-153
  semiotics 121
  social history 103, 106-108
  social information 118, 122, 126, 133, 135, 137
  subjectivity 117-121, 123, 129, 132-139
  technology 102-103, 110, 114
  theory 102
  transparency 123-124
  users 122
  See also Brothman, Brien; Cook, Terry; Heald,

Carolyn; Ketelaar, Eric; MacNeil, Heather

R

von Ranke, Leopold 15-16, 145, 155, 157
See also History "as it happened"

Records
bulk 79
destruction of 76, 84
mechanical reproductions of 48
types of 30, 42-43, 79
multiple copies of See *duplication*
See also Definitions of records, Dutch Manual, *Manual of Archive Administration, A*, *Modern Archives: Principles and Techniques*, Questioning Paradigm

Reinforcement paradigm
See *Manual of Archive Administration, A*

Respect des fonds *2, 7, 32-34, 37-38, 78, 125, 128, 133*

van Riemsdijk, Theodoor 23

Roosevelt, Franklin Delano 71

S

Schellenberg, Theodore Roosevelt 30, 65, 69-99
professional history 75-77
See also Conflict between Jenkinson and Schellenberg's theories, *Modern Archives: Principles and Techniques*

Schlesinger, Jr., Arthur 73
Scott, Joan Wallach 106
Smith, Adam 45
Society of American Archivists 76, 113
Space exploration 72-73
Stone, Lawrence 109
Study of history, The
"as it happened" 26, 118, 145
empricism 59, 147
in Great Britain 44-47, 59
intellectual history 153
local history 45-46
military history 45-46
objectivity 156
positivism 46, 73
postmodern history 109, 152
relativism 73, 147
scientific history 73, 84
social history 45, 59, 103, 106-108, 149
solidarity 73
statistical analysis 104

Q

Questioning paradigm 101-141
 administrative aspects 119
 appraisal 111, 124, 129, 135-136, 139-140, 152-153
 archives 101, 111, 117, 140
 communication 117, 122, 151
 context 102-103, 126, 135-136, 156
 critical theory 101-102, 105-106, 126-127, 139, 151
 cultural aspects 119-120, 130-131, 133, 150, 156
 definition of records 110-111, 124-127
 definition of the archive 151
 diversity 106, 113, 151, 156
 fonds 117, 121, 135
 electronic records 104, 110, 119
 historical orientation 101, 121-122, 127-128, 131
 historiography 105, 108-109
 identity 130
 inherited practice 127-128
 interpretation 101, 117-118, 122, 124-125, 134, 139, 155
 memory 106, 111, 126, 135
 metanarrative 105, 117
 narrative 131, 136
 objectivity 118, 121-122, 132-139
 paradigm change 102, 111-112, 118, 151
 poetics 119
 postmodern critical theory 104-105, 108, 114, 117-118, 120-124, 139-140, 152
 power 125, 127, 130, 134, 137-138
 records creators 134
 role of the archivist 103, 119, 121, 125, 130-132, 151-153
 semiotics 121
 social history 103, 106-108
 social information 118, 122, 126, 133, 135, 137
 subjectivity 117-121, 123, 129, 132-139
 technology 102-103, 110, 114
 theory 102
 transparency 123-124
 users 122
 See also Brothman, Brien; Cook, Terry; Heald,

Carolyn; Ketelaar, Eric; MacNeil, Heather

R

von Ranke, Leopold 15-16, 145, 155, 157
  See also History "as it happened"
Records
  bulk 79
  destruction of 76, 84
  mechanical reproductions of 48
  types of 30, 42-43, 79
    multiple copies of See duplication
  See also Definitions of records, Dutch Manual, *Manual of Archive Administration, A, Modern Archives: Principles and Techniques*, Questioning Paradigm
Reinforcement paradigm
  See *Manual of Archive Administration, A*
Respect des fonds *2, 7, 32-34, 37-38, 78, 125, 128, 133*
van Riemsdijk, Theodoor 23
Roosevelt, Franklin Delano 71

S

Schellenberg, Theodore Roosevelt 30, 65, 69-99
  professional history 75-77
  See also Conflict between Jenkinson and Schellenberg's theories, *Modern Archives: Principles and Techniques*
Schlesinger, Jr., Arthur 73
Scott, Joan Wallach 106
Smith, Adam 45
Society of American Archivists 76, 113
Space exploration 72-73
Stone, Lawrence 109
Study of history, The
  "as it happened" 26, 118, 145
  empricism 59, 147
  in Great Britain 44-47, 59
  intellectual history 153
  local history 45-46
  military history 45-46
  objectivity 156
  positivism 46, 73
  postmodern history 109, 152
  relativism 73, 147
  scientific history 73, 84
  social history 45, 59, 103, 106-108, 149
  solidarity 73
  statistical analysis 104

subjectivity 63-65, 109, 155-156
truth 124
See also Historiography, Influence of historiography, United Kingdom, United States
de Stuers, Victor 22-23

T

Technology
changes 7-8, 25, 64, 148, 153, 158-160
communications 11-13, 159
during World War I 11-12, 42-43, 64-65
during World War II 12, 148
See also Computers in archives, Electronic records, Typewriters
Tilly, Louise 106
Trevelyan, George 46
Typewriters 43, 103, 158-159
See also Technology

U

United Kingdom
archives 45-49, 51, 146, 154
British Public Records Office 47-48
British Records Association 48
county record offices 47
county record societies 45
General Registry Office 46-47
government 43-44
historians 44-46, 150
local history 45-46
military history 45
social history 45
United States
archives 69-99, 112-113, 138, 149-150, 154
broker state in government 71
Civil War 79
Farm Security Administration 71
Federal Records Act 89
G.I. Bill of Rights 72
House Un-American Activities Committee 74
National Archives 74-75, 80-82, 86, 89
National Labor Relations Act 72
New Deal 71-72
Office of Price Administration 76
Social Security Act 72
Tennessee Valley Authority 71
War Production Board 76
Works Progress Administration 71

V

Vital Center, The 73

W

Wealth of Nations, The 45-46
White, Hayden V. 108
Wisconsin Death Trip 109
Women, Work, and Family 106
Work of Art in the Age of Mechanical Reproduction 64
World War I 39-40, 42-45, 48-49, 79, 146, 154
See also Technology during World War I
World War II 60, 64, 71, 79, 147, 156
 See also Technology during World War II

About the Author

John Ridener holds a BA in American Studies, with an emphasis in the history and literature of the United States, from Hampshire College in Amherst, Massachusetts and an MLIS from San Jose State University. He currently works at the Earth Sciences and Map Library at the University of California, Berkeley where he specializes in map cataloging, digital resources, and geographic information systems. His research and academic interests include the cataloging of non-textual library material, visual presentation and navigation of geographic information, critical theory within archival and library contexts, and the convergence of physical geography, psychogeography, and art.

When not writing about archival theory or learning about geographical information systems and digital mapping, John's interests include listening to and creating experimental electronic music, playing baritone saxophone, reading: especially history, theory, and, more recently, child development books, and using bicycles in place of a family car. He lives in Oakland, California with his wife and daughter.

www.ingramcontent.com/pod-product-compliance
Lightning Source LLC
Chambersburg PA
CBHW021355300426
44114CB00012B/1235